Wildly Romantic

The English Romantic Poets:

The Mad, the Bad, and the Dangerous

Catherine M. Andronik

Henry Holt and Company · New York

Art Credits

Use of the following paintings are courtesy of the Wordsworth Trust: p. 4, William Wordsworth; p. 29, Mrs. Coleridge; p. 60, Sara Coleridge; p. 64, Hartley Coleridge; p. 222, Edith Southey; p. 232, : Dora Wordsworth.

Use of the following paintings are courtesy of the National Portrait Gallery, London: p. 20, Samuel Taylor Coleridge, by Peter Vandyke; p. 38, William Wordsworth, by Benjamin Robert Haydon; p. 45, Samuel Taylor Coleridge, by Washington Allston; p. 76, George Gordon Byron, 6th Baron Byron, by Thomas Phillips; p. 122, George Gordon Byron, 6th Baron Byron, by Henry Hoppner Meyer; p. 127, Lady Caroline Lamb, by Eliza H. Trotter; p. 131, Anne Isabella, Lady Byron, by Samuel Freeman; p. 140, Percy Bysshe Shelley, by Amelia Curran; p. 144, George Gordon Byron, 6th Baron Byron, by Richard Westall; p. 146, Mary Wollstonecraft Shelley [questionable identity], by Samuel John Stump; p. 152, John Keats, by Joseph Severn; p. 220, Robert Southey, by Edward Nash; p. 226, Edith May Southey and Sara Coleridge, by Edward Nash; p. 240, William Wordsworth, by Benjamin Robert Haydon.

Use of the following paintings are courtesy of the Bodleian Library, Oxford University, Albinger Collection/Shelley Collection: p. 92, Percy Bysshe Shelley (Shelley as a Boy); p. 110, Mary Shelley, by Reginald Easton.

Use of the painting on p. 188, Allegra Byron [questionable identity], is courtesy of the Russell-Cotes Art Gallery & Museum, England.

Use of the painting on p. 204, The Funeral of Shelley, by Louis-Edouard Fournier, is courtesy of the Walker Art Gallery, National Museums Liverpool.

Henry Holt and Company, LLC
Publishers since 1866
175 Fifth Avenue
New York, New York 10010
www.henryholtchildrensbooks.com

Henry Holt® is a registered trademark of Henry Holt
and Company, LLC.

Library of Congress Cataloging-in-Publication Data
Andronik, Catherine M.
Wildly romantic : the English Romantic poets—the mad, the bad, and the
dangerous / Catherine M. Andronik.—1st ed.
p.   cm.
Includes bibliographical references and index.
ISBN-13: 978-0-8050-7783-4 / ISBN-10: 0-8050-7783-9
1. Poets, English—19th century—Biography—Juvenile literature.
2. Romanticism—Great Britian—Juvenile literature.   I. Title.
PR590.A53 2007
821'.709—dc22 [B]   2006018227

First Edition—2007
Book designed by Amelia May Anderson
Printed in the United States of America on acid-free paper. ∞

10 9 8 7 6 5 4 3 2 1

For Mr. Flory, Mrs. Porter, and Mr. Creeger—
teachers who knew the power of words

CONTENTS

INTRODUCTION

They were revolutionary days. Technology was changing and developing so fast, people could barely keep up with it. Machines were taking over jobs that had been done for generations by a pair of strong hands guided by a creative mind. Unemployment rates were on their way up. So were prices for essentials like food and housing. The government seemed to care only about itself. Discontent was high. Rebellion—even war—was breaking out everywhere.

And in rebellious days, there are rebellious people.

One was a political revolutionary in his younger days, and a revolutionary in a different way when he grew a bit older. People who knew him as an adult never suspected that there was a little girl out there who called him "daddy"—in another language.

His closest friend wanted to found a commune out in the wilderness as soon as he got out of college. He was convincing enough to get a few others to stake their lives on the idea. Wives—his included—were part of the deal. He was brilliant, multifaceted, and fascinated by the supernatural. He was also sinking into the inexorable whirlpool of drug addiction.

The two friends were sure they could change the world—or at least the way people wrote and thought about the world—through their words. Their collaboration created something new and exciting, something people had never really seen before.

And they attracted followers who liked the whole idea of

revolution and changing the world through a powerful new way of weaving words.

One lived a Cinderella story. But for him, there was no happily-ever-after ending. Women, from the wives and daughters of friends right down to his own sister, threw themselves at him. And he took advantage of them for all they were worth. He left behind a trail of lovers, broken lives, and broken hearts, male and female alike. His life was the epitome of scandal. He lived to shock. He was hounded out of his native land in disgrace. When life gave him lemons, he made very lucrative lemonade—he turned the scandals into stories. And, meanwhile, he burned with a determination to save a country.

Then there was the atheist, the pyromaniac, the polygamist wannabe drawn to teenage jailbait. He tried to turn his writing talents toward revolutionary politics. He had a fatal attraction to the untamed power of the ocean. In the hindsight of history, his second wife has probably upstaged him.

And there was the dreamy little guy from the wrong side of the tracks. He wrote like an angel and found the love of his life. Things were looking good for him—until a deadly, incurable disease dropped him like a stone.

Literature—especially poetry—has never been the same since these people pushed their way into history like a force of nature.

Are these the Beat poets of the 1950s? Hippies of the '60s? Singer-songwriters just a generation past?

They're older than any of these. They're the English Romantic poets of the early 1800s, writers who believed that poetry should express strong feelings in language that was as close as possible to the way ordinary people spoke. The most important among them were William Wordsworth, Samuel Taylor Coleridge, Lord Byron, Percy Bysshe Shelley, and John Keats.

One bunch of wildly Romantic guys.

William Wordsworth

WORDSWORTH

"The Child Is Father to the Man"

If his mother had lived, William Wordsworth's life would have been much different. It was a story that would be repeated for almost all the major poets of the eighteenth century, though more often it was the father who died. If Wordsworth's mother had lived, William would have grown up in a huge, comfortable home, courtesy of the landowner Sir James Lowther. John Wordsworth, William's father, worked for Lowther as a sort of legal adviser (in addition to being the area's coroner). William probably would not have spent his boyhood in the English Lake District he would come to love; would not have glided, alone and silent except for the hiss of his skates, along the frozen lakes; would not have called at dusk to the owls in the trees and heard them answer. The fateful meetings in his life—with Annette

Vallon, with Samuel Taylor Coleridge—might never have happened. He might have had the heart and soul of a poet; he might have grown up to love words. But, as Wordsworth himself would one day write, "the child is father to the man." If his mother had lived, the images and events that shaped the poetry of the man would not have been part of the experiences of the child.

The heart and soul of the poet emerged when William was a teenager. As a child, though, he had the heart and soul of a brat. Every child throws tantrums. William's were a bit extreme. He once ripped up a family portrait with an old fencing sword—then threatened to kill himself with the same blade. His mother, Ann, said that of all her children, it was William's fate that worried her the most.

But while her children were quite young, Ann Wordsworth took a trip from her home in Cockermouth in the north of England to visit a friend in London. Her friend put her up in the best bedroom the family had to offer. You can only imagine what the worst bedroom must have been like, because the one Ann settled into was cold and damp, with a stiff draft blowing into the windows. Ann died of pneumonia soon afterward. Her husband was not prepared to raise small children by himself, so they were separated, sent to live with various relatives. It would be nine years before William saw one of his brothers again, after the death of their father (also, coincidentally, from pneumonia following a cold, wet journey).

Young William was lucky. He was sent to a school in England's Lake District, whose wild atmosphere spoke to his restless, outdoorsy, sensitive soul. In summer he could walk about the fells, the rocky, rolling hills between the region's beautiful glacial lakes. In winter he learned to skate on those same lakes, frozen as clear and solid as glass. The curriculum at the school was traditional, but its headmaster wasn't; he was fond of modern poetry and kept a rich and up-to-date library.

William himself tried his hand at writing poetry when he was about fourteen, and even managed to get a piece printed in a magazine in 1787. He liked to compose poems as he walked, memorizing the words he'd put together until he reached a place where he could get pen and paper and write them down. Since he was always trudging around the lanes and hills anyway, he made a convenient dog-walker for friends and neighbors. One of the dogs learned to alert William to those potentially awkward moments when a passerby might find a young man muttering to himself threatening. When another person came into view, the dog would stop and stare at William until he got the message and shut up.

Mumbling poetry to himself—it was a habit William Words-worth never outgrew. At an inn where Wordsworth, now an adult, had been a guest, the innkeeper remembered that odd man whose "hobby was poetry . . . mumbling to hissel' along t'roads."

When it came time to think about continuing his education, William was accepted as a sizar, a scholarship student, into St. John's College, Cambridge University. And the following sum-mer, he was reunited at last with his sister Dorothy. She and Mary Hutchinson, a girl the Wordsworth children had known since childhood, came to visit William. They spent the summer tramping across the countryside on foot. Walking was a major mode of transportation in the 1800s. But in William's case, it was more of an extreme sport. Anyone connected with William Wordsworth had to be an untiring walker. A few summers later, William and a school friend walked through France, Switzerland, and Italy—including the Alps—on foot, packs on their heads, covering fifteen miles before breakfast. By the end of their trip they had totaled over two thousand miles.

William started college with excellent grades. Four years later, he graduated without honors or recognition of any kind. The young men around him were more interested in their social life than academics. Sometimes they would start dressing for a midafternoon dinner an hour early, go from dinner to a string of parties, and only then, in the wee hours of the morning, return to their rooms to read or study. They woke up late, missing classes. And William Wordsworth was one of the boys.

When the French first started pressing for greater liberty and equality for the lower classes, it sounded like a wonderful idea to the English, especially the younger people. What teenager *doesn't* like the idea of being free *and* equal to authority? Twice William would cross the English Channel to France during revolutionary years, in search of the common people. His life so far had convinced him that the truest answers to what life was all about lay not with the rich and famous, the sort of people he'd gone to university with, but with people who worked hard and lived simply, farmers and craftsmen. The whole idea of the

French Revolution really hit home for him when he was walking along a road one day with an old soldier. They saw a peasant, emaciated and dressed in rags, and William's companion turned to him and said, " 'Tis against *that* which we are fighting."

In England, William wrote essays in the form of letters that would have gotten him thrown into prison if he'd actually published them. They spoke against the nobility and criticized a government that spent lavishly but disregarded the poverty so many people endured in the countryside or in the overcrowded slums of the growing cities. When King Louis XVI went to the guillotine in France, William approved; it was a necessary death in the cause of liberty. When England passed laws forbidding liberal-thinking groups to meet, William wrote against the laws.

And then he met Annette Vallon. She didn't speak English. His French was shaky at best, and his English was so deeply gutteral, with the strong accent of the northern part of the country, that she probably couldn't have understood much of what he said even if she *had* spoken the language. Life in Revolutionary France was all about "Liberty, Equality, Fraternity." William and Annette certainly shared liberty and fraternity in their short time together. But as for equality, nine months later, with William back in England and the unrest of the Terror shaking France to its roots, Annette was alone in the town of Blois registering the birth of a daughter, Caroline. The baby's father's name was recorded as William Wordswodth. The child's existence was kept secret from all but the immediate family of "Wordswodth" for over a hundred years.

William may have wanted to return to France when he learned that he was a father—there is some evidence he even went, dangerous as it was once the Terror struck and anyone remotely aristocratic could be sentenced to death. Annette apparently believed that her lover would marry her. But as the years passed, the three grew older and moved on with lives that took other directions.

University had been enjoyable. Tramping about Europe and the north of England (and meeting at least one willing young woman) had been entertaining. Spinning out poetry during long walks was fun. But now it was time for William to settle down and find a way to make a living. There was really only one way for a young unmarried man who wanted to be a writer and was not independently wealthy to survive. That was to find himself a patron, a rich gentleman who thought highly enough of his writing to give him an annual allowance. It was like getting a grant from a foundation today. The money was usually just enough to pay for rented lodgings and basic needs, so the writer would have time to concentrate on his craft instead of survival. For William, salvation came in the person of Raisley Calvert. Calvert was only about William's age, but their circumstances were very different. For one, Calvert was rich. For another, he was suffering from tuberculosis and didn't have long to live. He thought William showed promise as a writer. William was Calvert's dutiful companion in his last days. When he died, he left the poet the grand sum of nine hundred pounds. Today, that amount would barely rent a studio apartment in London for a month. In the late 1700s, it was enough to live on quite comfortably for a very long time.

William was getting help from other friends as well. He was living in London and offering his services as a tutor. Like Raisley Calvert, Wordsworth's students had great hopes for their teacher. Being from families with much more money than Wordsworth's, they were able to pay the rent for him on a house called Racedown, in England's West Country. William had a special affinity for the West Country. Not long before, he'd been walking near the ancient monument of Stonehenge. When a sudden hailstorm struck, he took shelter among the fallen and leaning monoliths and had a mystical experience of going back in time to the weird circle's origins. He wrote,

While through those vestiges of ancient times
I ranged, and by the solitude o'ercome,
I had a reverie and saw the past,
Saw multitudes of men, and here and there,
A single Briton in his wolf-skin vest
With shield and stone-axe, stride across the Wold;
The voice of spears was heard, the rattling spear
Shaken by arms of mighty bone, in strength
Long mouldered of barbaric majesty.
I called upon the darkness; and it took,
A midnight darkness seemed to come and take
All objects from my sight; and lo! again
The desart visible by dismal flames!

It is the sacrificial Altar, fed
With living men; how deep the groans; the voice
Of those in the gigantic wicker thrills
Throughout the region far and near, pervades
The monumental hillocks; and the pomp
Is for both worlds, the living and the dead.

Like any homeowner just starting out, as soon as he moved into Racedown, William began ordering the necessities for his new life. Shoes, for instance. And not just any shoes: six pairs, two for dress and four with thick double soles and sturdy leather uppers. William was planning on doing a lot of walking.

Moving into Racedown was important to William for another reason. He had never gotten over how his brothers and sisters had been separated when they were so young. His sister Dorothy had never married. She called herself "dimunitive Dolly" because of her height—or lack thereof, since she was just five feet tall. One of her eyes didn't look quite right. She was bright and capable and a wonderful companion, but not a good-looking girl. By the time she'd turned thirty, she realized "it would be absurd at my age to talk of marriage." There weren't many alternatives for unmarried women at the time. She had been working as a housekeeper for a relative. She even met the king and queen while at that job. But she was unhappy. Once William had Racedown to call home, Dorothy was able to move in with him, which suited both of them perfectly.

Also living with the Wordsworths at Racedown was a little

boy named Basil Montagu, the two-year-old son of a friend. Wordsworth had offered to be Basil's tutor in an unusual kind of schooling. Many intellectuals were fascinated by the ideas of the philosopher Jean-Jacques Rousseau, who wrote that Nature was a far better teacher than the formal education system. Like many of their contemporaries, Wordsworth and little Basil Montagu's father (who was also named Basil) were part of the circle of a philosopher named William Godwin while they were living in London. Godwin claimed that mankind was naturally good and needed only to allow that goodness free rein. Basil Montagu would be taught by these principles. Sometimes, though, such lofty ideals were hard to put into practice with a live, lively child. When he would throw tantrums, Basil would be locked alone in a room at Racedown—not because it was recommended by any of the philosophers whose advice the Wordsworths were follow-ing but, as Dorothy wrote, "because the noise was unpleasant to us." The Wordsworths had a maid, Peggy, who took care of the house, and sometimes found herself taking care of Basil as well. Rousseau hadn't mentioned nannies.

Then Racedown had another long-term visitor: the Words-worths' childhood friend, Mary Hutchinson. Her sister had just died of tuberculosis, and Mary had been her companion to the end. The care of a relative dying of "consumption" was some-thing many families went through in the late 1700s and early 1800s. It was a draining, exhausting experience, both physically and emotionally, especially since little was known about the disease, common though it was. Mary needed time to rest, recuperate, and regain her strength, and for six months she was a welcome guest in the Wordsworths' home.

Then, in June of 1797, just around the time Mary left, a visitor came to Racedown who would change the Wordsworths' lives forever. He and William were writers, and they had already met briefly, exchanged letters, and recognized each other as kindred spirits. Dorothy Wordsworth was outdoors when the visitor, still outside the fence that surrounded Racedown's fields, saw her in the distance. And, though he had already walked forty miles (they truly were kindred spirits), he leaped over a gate and came plowing through the corn like a force of nature. His name was Samuel Taylor Coleridge.

The Poems

And in the frosty season, when the sun
Was set, and visible for many a mile
The cottage windows blazed through twilight gloom,
I heeded not their summons: happy time
It was indeed for all of us—for me
It was a time of rapture! Clear and loud
The village clock tolled six—I wheeled about,
Proud and exulting, like an untired horse
That cares not for his home. All shod with steel,
We hissed along the polished ice in games
Confederate, imitative of the chase
And woodland pleasures—the resounding horn,
The pack loud chiming, and the hunted hare.
So through the darkness and the cold we flew,
And not a voice was idle; with the din
Smitten, the precipices rang aloud;
The leafless trees and every icy crag
Tinkled like iron; while far distant hills
Into the tumult sent an alien sound
Of melancholy not unnoticed, while the stars

Eastward were sparkling clear, and in the west

The orange sky of evening died away.

Not seldom from the uproar I retired

Into a silent bay, or sportively

Glanced sideway, leaving the tumultuous throng,

To cut across the reflex of a star

That fled, and, flying still before me, gleamed

Upon the glassy plain; and oftentimes,

When we had given our bodies to the wind,

And all the shadowy banks on either side

Came sweeping through the darkness, spinning still

The rapid line of motion, then at once

Have I, reclining back upon my heels,

Stopped short; yet still the solitary cliffs

Wheeled by me—even as if the earth had rolled

With visible motion her diurnal round!

Behind me did they stretch in solemn train,

Feebler and feebler, and I stood and watched

Till all was tranquil as a dreamless sleep.

from THE PRELUDE, BOOK XI

(The French Revolution as it appeared to enthusiasts at its commencement)

O pleasant exercise of hope and joy!

For mighty were the auxiliars which then stood

Upon our side, us who were strong in love!

Bliss was it in that dawn to be alive,

But to be young was very Heaven! O times,

In which the meager, stale, forbidding ways

Of custom, law, and statute, took at once

The attraction of a country in romance!

When Reason seemed the most to assert her rights

When most intent on making of herself

A prime enchantress—to assist the work,

Which then was going forward in her name!

Not favoured spots alone, but the whole Earth,

The beauty wore of promise—that which sets

(As at some moments might not be unfelt

Among the bowers of Paradise itself)

The budding rose above the rose full blown.

What temper at the prospect did not wake

To happiness unthought of? The inert

Were roused, and lively natures rapt away!

They who had fed their childhood upon dreams,

The playfellows of fancy, who had made

All powers of swiftness, subtlety, and strength

Their ministers—who in lordly wise had stirred

Among the grandest objects of the sense,
And dealt with whatsoever they found there
As if they had within some lurking right
To wield it—they, too, who of gentle mood
Had watched all gentle motions, and to these
Had fitted their own thoughts, schemers more mild,
And in the region of their peaceful selves—
Now was it that *both* found, the meek and lofty
Did both find helpers to their hearts' desire,
And stuff at hand, plastic as they could wish—
Were called upon to exercise their skill,
Not in Utopia, subterranean fields,
Or some secreted island, Heaven knows where!
But in this very world, which is the world
Of all of us—the place where, in the end,
We find our happiness, or not at all!

Samuel Taylor Coleridge

ESTEESI

"To Begin My Tale"

$\mathcal{T}$hey say that the youngest child runs with his emotions and desires. When two-year-old Samuel Taylor Coleridge—the youngest of *ten* children—was taken to the family doctor for a shot, the doctor covered the boy's eyes so he wouldn't have to see the needle go into his skin. And little Sam (who hated that name) screamed, as most two-year-olds would. Then the doctor realized Sam wasn't screaming in fear: He wanted his eyes open. He *wanted* to watch—and did, fascinated.

Five years later, Sam and his brother Francis got into an argument, a pretty silly argument, especially considering Francis was already a teenager and the issue was a piece of cheese they both wanted. Sam, just a fraction of his older brother's size, grabbed a kitchen knife and chased him with it. When he realized how naughty he'd been, Sam ran away and hid along the banks of the nearby River Otter. The family went out searching for him, unsuccessfully. Little Sam must have hidden *very* well. He ended up staying out in the open all night. As far as that sensitive seven-year-old was concerned, he was being punished, and his punishment was abandonment.

Life did not get easier for young Sam. His father was a vicar—a clergyman—in the town of Ottery St. Mary in Devonshire, in the West Country. John Coleridge was a man with wide interests, broad curiosity, and strong opinions. He did a bit of writing, not just on religious subjects but also about that revolution going on over in the colonies (he was against it). He knew a little about astronomy, and sometimes he would take his youngest son aside at night for some stargazing, sharing his child's sense of wonder. Samuel would later recall, "I never thought as a child." That came from being the youngest of ten children, too.

John Coleridge was already fifty-three years old when his last child was born. In 1781, when Francis entered the Royal Navy, John had a premonition that he would never see his son again. Soon after, he suffered a fatal heart attack. The Coleridges had to leave their home at the vicarage.

Samuel was sent away to school—not a good boarding school, but Christ's Hospital in London. It was a charity school for the sons of poor clergymen. Every day for three years, he and six hundred other boys rose from their iron dormitory beds at six, dressed in drab blue uniforms, ate a sorry bowl of thin porridge, and hoped to avoid the schoolmasters' floggings. When he wasn't at school, Samuel lived with an uncle, who saw nothing inappropriate about taking his young nephew along when he went to the tavern. Later in Samuel's life, some of the Christ's Hospital boys—Charles Lamb, Leigh Hunt—would re-enter his life as literary men.

Books like *Robinson Crusoe* and *The Arabian Nights* were among the few bright spots in young Coleridge's life. Reading was a way for him to escape from his bleak surroundings. The city must have seemed especially stifling after a childhood in the Coleridges' country home, surrounded by intelligent adult conversation and a natural world to observe. One day Samuel was on his way down a crowded London street, waving his arms as he acted out a scene from a Greek myth he'd been reading—Leander swimming across the Hellespont to visit his beloved. He was an accident waiting to happen. At first, the gentleman he smacked in the side was convinced that the world's clumsiest pickpocket was after his wallet. But Samuel began to apologize and explain. The gentleman was so impressed by the boy's obvious love of literature, he handed him a treasure: a ticket for the local lending library, which entitled him to borrow two books at a time. There was no such thing as a public library back then; libraries were available only to the people who gave them money, not to charity-case ragamuffins like Samuel Taylor Coleridge. Books made up for the mediocre education Samuel was getting at Christ's Hospital. It didn't help that his teachers were oblivious to the young genius in their midst. To them, Sam Coleridge was not the sharpest knife in the drawer—until one found him reading Virgil, in the original Latin, just for fun.

Coleridge won a scholarship to Cambridge University, where he was a classmate of William Wordsworth's younger brother Christopher. By then he was doing a lot of writing and winning awards for some of it. But he was also still the impulsive baby of the family. He tried whatever college life had to offer, good or bad, and, like many young men in college, he hadn't learned his limits. One night he jumped into the River Cam for a swim—without bothering to take his clothes off. Afterward, he fell straight into his bed, again without taking his now soaking wet clothes off. He paid for his midnight dip by becoming ill with rheumatic fever.

The treatment for just about everything at the time was an exciting wonder drug called opium, taken dissolved in liquid. It calmed upset patients, eased their pain, helped them rest and sleep while they recuperated. The only negative effects were in those weak-willed individuals who couldn't stop taking the drug, or an opium-alcohol mixture called laudanum, when their medical treatment was over. Young Coleridge didn't know yet whether he would be one of these unfortunates.

In addition to taking his opium like a good patient, he was drinking, as many of his college associates did, and nights in the local taverns could get expensive. He was also an easy target for people like the scam artist who promised to decorate his room—for an up-front fee—and then disappeared. Coleridge tried to win his cash back playing the lottery, but just lost more. He was twenty-one years old, temptations like opium and alcohol and gambling coming at him from every side, and his life was spiraling out of control.

So he disappeared. It took his brother George four months to track him down. People were talking about the unusual young man, Silas Tomkyn Comberbache, who had signed up with the 15th Light Dragoons, a cavalry unit, back in December of 1793. He just didn't fit the mold of a typical soldier. The stories this young man told at night to entertain the soldiers were classical myths. When a listener mangled a quote in Greek, the lowly recruit corrected him flawlessly. For four months Silas, who couldn't ride a horse and was useless in the cavalry, had been doing odd jobs such as mucking out the stables, helping illiterate soldiers write love letters, and nursing the sick. And he was no coward, this Silas. For eight days he'd been assigned to the dreaded "Pest House," taking care of a dragoon dying of smallpox. In their foul, tiny cabin, the two had been completely quarantined from the rest of the regiment. Food and water were left at the door for Silas to bring inside when the coast was clear. His patient recovered. And, amazingly, Nurse Silas never contracted the highly contagious disease.

The Coleridge brothers paid the army to release Silas from his duties. He was discharged on April 10, 1794; the reason listed was insanity.

The family's next step was to get their youngest brother back into university—this time, Oxford. But Samuel Taylor Coleridge had a few more wild ideas up his sleeve, and at Oxford he found a worthy partner in crime: Robert Southey.

Robert Southey's childhood made Coleridge's seem normal and even idyllic in comparison. He was born in 1774, two years after Coleridge, to a poor family in Bristol. But the family had a rich relation, an aunt named Elizabeth Tyler, who offered to give the boy advantages his own father couldn't. Tyler may have been rich, but she didn't know much about raising children. Until he was six years old, Robert and his aunt slept together in the same bed. Not only that, but he was not allowed to get up until she did. He would wake at daybreak; she stayed in bed until nearly noon. He spent the long hours absolutely still, staring at the ceiling. Once he was up and about, he was forbidden to play in the garden. There was *dirt* out there, out of the question for well-brought-up little boys.

Robert finally rebelled when he got to school. He was expelled for a piece he wrote for the Westminster School magazine opposing the common punishment of flogging. Now Aunt Elizabeth was paying her nephew's way through Oxford, hoping he'd settle down and become something respectable, like a minister.

Coleridge and Southey got to talking one day about the perfect way to live. Before long, their dreamy conversation took on a life of its own, and they actually started to believe they could make it happen. The plan was that they'd buy a piece of farmland in America. At first they liked the idea of Kentucky, but then Coleridge heard about the Susquehanna River in Pennsylvania, fell in love with the name, and started considering real estate there. And he was serious. He was doing what today we'd call relocation research: how much did land cost, was it good for farming, how long and hard were the winters, what were the neighbors like? He estimated that if they could get twelve men and twelve women interested in the idea, it would cost each about 125 pounds to charter a ship, purchase provisions, and sail to Pennsylvania. Southey was sure his aunt would help the group out with money, too.

Once Coleridge, Southey, and any other friends they could talk into their scheme arrived in Paradise on the Susquehanna, their plan was to found a "pantisocracy," a society where every man took an equal part in governing. It would be a farming community run by thinkers and writers and poets. No single person in the group would own property. All land and goods would be held jointly, a concept Coleridge referred to as *aspheterism*. And there, Southey wrote, "When Coleridge and I are sawing down a tree, we shall discuss metaphysics; criticize poetry when hunting a buffalo, and write sonnets whilst following the plough." They figured the men would only have to do manual labor about three hours a day to make the operation a success, which left plenty of time to think and talk and write. It did cross Southey's mind that he, Coleridge, and their interested friends knew nothing about farming beyond the fact that it was done outdoors in the heart of Nature, where they thought they wanted to be. Southey volunteered to spend time on a farm in Wales before the group sailed to America, where he was sure to learn enough to get by. (This from the man who had grown up forbidden to touch dirt.) Or, even better, they'd bring along some extra people to do the real work. The servants would take care of the log splitting and house building and plowing and harvesting. This idea solved many problems—but then a debate started over whether the scheme could still be called a pantisocracy, since servants certainly weren't in a class to take part in governing along with gentlemen.

The pantisocracy was Romantic in its ideas of getting back to Nature and living self-sufficiently off the land while thinking deep thoughts—but it was romantic in the other way, too. The Fricker family, from the fashionable city of Bath, had five sisters: Sarah, Edith, Mary, Martha, and Elizabeth. Their father had been a successful businessman, or so they thought, and they had enjoyed a comfortable life. Then he went bankrupt. The sisters took jobs as seamstresses, although Mary had dreams of becoming an actress. Sarah worked for a while for Robert Southey's mother, and later for his late-rising, dirt-hating genteel aunt, Elizabeth Tyler, who wanted to help the destitute young sisters. Through Southey, the Frickers got to know Coleridge and the other gentlemen the boys had drawn into the pantisocracy scheme. Before long, the Fricker sisters were part of the bait: Join the pantisocrats, and you'd get a nice little piece of farmland in America *and* a wife in the bargain. Not only would there be servants to do the farming, there would now be women, who would have plenty of time to take care of the cooking and housework, since all babies do is sleep, or so the men reasoned. There was even a bit of talk about swapping spouses and of raising children just as the group owned land, communally.

The Fricker girls didn't exactly refuse. Sarah was paired up with Coleridge. Edith's promised partner was Southey. Mary married a friend of Southey's, Robert Lovell.

Mrs. Coleridge

Martha's catch was to be another pantisocrat, George Burnett. Southey's dog, Rover, was also an official pantisocrat, but there is no record of his owner's having chosen him a mate, Fricker or otherwise.

Elizabeth Tyler had been supporting her nephew while he was at university. She was also helping out the Fricker sisters. But when she got wind of the pantisocracy scheme, she'd had enough. In the middle of a cold, rainy October night, she threw Robert Southey out of her house with only the clothes on his back. The two pairs of young lovers, Southey and Edith, Coleridge and Sarah, ran away together to Wales.

On October 4, 1795, Sarah Fricker—Sally Pally to her

fiancé—married her Esteesi (as in S. T. C.) with her mother as witness. No one from the Coleridge family came to the wedding, and whenever Coleridge visited his family within the next few months, Sarah didn't accompany him. They made an unlikely couple, he a big, lumbering man with a "carcase of a face," his mouth always slightly open because he had difficulty breathing through his nose, his Devonshire accent strong and broad, she petite, with a mane of beautiful auburn-brown hair, her manner sophisticated and chic. The young couple started out with a nearly empty rented cottage. The only piece of furniture in it was a bed. Almost immediately after they moved in, Coleridge contacted a friend to bring him some necessities: food, a tea-kettle, a dustpan, a carpet—and an Aeolian windharp to hang on the door.

As for finances, a man named Thomas Poole admired what he'd seen of Coleridge's writing and became his patron, agreeing to give the young poet forty pounds a year for seven years. It wasn't much for the newlyweds to survive on.

In 1797, the Coleridges moved into a cottage in Nether Stowey, the last little house on Lime Street before the poorhouse. In fact, the poorhouse was probably in better condition than the cottage. It was falling apart and crawling with mice, which Coleridge just didn't have the heart to kill. There was no heat, and there was an open fireplace instead of an oven to cook in. Visitors would often find the Coleridges' wet laundry spread out around the fireplace to dry. Outside the front door was a gutter where the trash from the other houses in the village flowed to the bottom of Lime Street. In back was a plot of weeds that passed for a garden, with just enough room for a pigsty. Sarah was keeping the budget to sixteen shillings a week. Between Thomas Poole's patronage and a handful of writing jobs, her husband wasn't always able to provide even that little amount. Sarah was not an especially organized housekeeper, so Coleridge tried to set up a schedule to help both of them do the daily chores. It didn't work.

During the winter in that drafty, unheated cottage, Coleridge suffered terrible aches and pains, especially in his face, and he was prone to toothaches. Everyone was thankful for the relief he got from that wonderful medicine, opium. But it did seem like he was taking more and more of it, and his behavior was strange when he was under its influence. He'd say such uncharacteristic things, write such peculiar letters, and sometimes produce such haunting images in the poetry he scribbled after dosing himself.

The pantisocracy dream was an idea whose time had come and gone. Edith Fricker finally married Robert Southey and went with him to Portugal to stay with his uncle. But her sister Mary Lovell, the first to marry a would-be pantisocrat, was soon a widow with a baby son to raise, dependent on her married sisters for help. Martha Fricker had wisely decided not to marry George Burnett, who, friends heard, died in 1811, having given his life up to opium after failing as a minister, a writer, and an army surgeon.

Before long, Sarah and Coleridge had their first child, a boy they named David Hartley. While home alone, Sarah went into labor with Hartley two weeks early and delivered him all by herself. The pantisocracy dream might have ended, but that didn't mean that Coleridge had given up on creative ideas for living a fulfilling life. Still, now he had a family to support, and there wasn't a lot of money coming in. Practicality—which he called "those two Giants, . . . BREAD & CHEESE"—was threatening to influence his decisions.

The private notebook Coleridge kept—his "flycatcher"—was full of his bright ideas. Maybe he'd spend some time in Germany, studying and translating German poetry. Maybe he'd actually get someone to compose music for the opera libretto he'd written, and they'd get it produced. Maybe he'd write an encyclopedia. Maybe he'd become a teacher, or even a clergyman. Maybe he'd write essays and poems.

One job Coleridge was actually doing and getting paid for was reviewing books, mainly the gothic novels that were the nineteenth century's answer to Stephen King. "Indeed," Coleridge commented, "I am almost weary of the Terrible . . . dungeons, and old castles, & solitary Houses by the Sea Side, & Caverns, & Woods, & extraordinary characters, & all the tribe of Horror & Mystery." (Notice he said "almost.") And he was writing poetry, at a rate of about fifty lines a day. But he wasn't popular or successful, and he "saw it plainly, that literature was not a profession by which I could expect to live."

Back in September of 1795, at a talk in Bristol for literary-minded gentlemen, Coleridge had met a fellow poet by the name of William Wordsworth. Occasionally the two exchanged letters after that. Then, in June 1797, Coleridge pulled on his good, sturdy, thick-soled walking shoes and set off across the hills and pastures surrounding Nether Stowey. When, after hours of walking, Racedown came into sight across a cornfield, there was only one fence left for him to jump.

The Poems

FROST AT MIDNIGHT

    The Frost performs its secret ministry,
Unhelped by any wind. The owlet's cry
Came loud—and hark, again! loud as before.
The inmates of my cottage, all at rest,
Have left me to that solitude, which suits
Abstruser musings: save that at my side
My cradled infant slumbers peacefully.
'Tis calm indeed! so calm, that it disturbs
And vexes meditation with its strange
And extreme silentness. Sea, hill, and wood,
This populous village! Sea, hill, and wood,
With all the numberless goings-on of life,
Inaudible as dreams! the thin blue flame
Lies on my low-burnt fire, and quivers not;
Only that film, which fluttered on the grate,
Still flutters there, the sole unquiet thing.
Methinks its motion in this hush of nature
Gives it dim sympathies with me who live,
Making it a companionable form,

Whose puny flaps and freaks the idling Spirit
By its own moods interprets, everywhere
Echo or mirror seeking of itself,
And makes a toy of Thought.
                But O! how oft,
How oft, at school, with most believing mind,
Presageful, have I gazed upon the bars,
To watch that fluttering *stranger!* and as oft
With unclosed lids, already had I dreamt
Of my sweet birthplace, and the old church tower,
Whose bells, the poor man's only music, rang
From morn to evening, all the hot fair-day,
So sweetly, that they stirred and haunted me
With a wild pleasure, falling on mine ear
Most like articulate sounds of things to come!
So gazed I, till the soothing things, I dreamt,
Lulled me to sleep, and sleep prolonged my dreams!
And so I brooded all the following morn,
Awed by the stern preceptor's face, mine eye
Fixed with mock study on my swimming book:
Save if the door half opened, and I snatched
A hasty glance, and still my heart leaped up,
For still I hoped to see the *stranger's* face,
Townsman, or aunt, or sister more beloved,
My playmate when we both were clothed alike!
   Dear Babe, that sleepest cradled by my side,

Whose gentle breathings, heard in this deep calm,
Fill up the intersperséd vacancies
And momentary pauses of the thought!
My babe so beautiful! it thrills my heart
With tender gladness, thus to look at thee,
And think that thou shalt learn far other lore,
And in far other scenes! For I was reared
In the great city, pent 'mid cloisters dim,
And saw nought lovely but the sky and stars.
But *thou*, my babe! shalt wander like a breeze
By lakes and sandy shores, beneath the crags
Of ancient mountain, and beneath the clouds,
Which image in their bulk both lakes and shores
And mountain crags: so shalt thou see and hear
The lovely shapes and sounds intelligible
Of that eternal language, which thy God
Utters, who from eternity doth teach
Himself in all, and all things in himself.
Great universal Teacher! he shall mold
Thy spirit, and by giving make it ask.

    Therefore all seasons shall be sweet to thee,
Whether the summer clothe the general earth
With greenness, or the redbreast sit and sing
Betwixt the tufts of snow on the bare branch
Of mossy apple tree, while the nigh thatch
Smokes in the sun-thaw; whether the eave-drops fall

Heard only in the trances of the blast,
Or if the secret ministry of frost
Shall hang them up in silent icicles,
Quietly shining to the quiet Moon.

William Wordsworth

LYRICAL BALLADEERS

"Only One Soul"

$\mathcal{I}$t started out as mutual professional admiration. It turned into a close and fateful friendship, and a landmark creative collaboration. When the relationship was at its height, Coleridge said that he, William, and Dorothy "were three people, but only one soul."

When Racedown became too small for Wordsworth and the company that seemed to snowball around him, he rented a larger house, not far away, called Alfoxden. There were nine rooms that could serve as bedrooms, plus three parlors for conversation with Coleridge and with the other freethinkers they were attracting.

Once again Wordsworth was living on the edge of a potential revolution, but this time it was unintentional. England was at war with France; for two days there was quite a stir as a handful of Frenchmen actually "invaded" the coast in a boat they'd sailed across the Channel. England was on the lookout for French spies, which meant any suspicious activity—and those people around Alfoxden and Nether Stowey were definitely suspicious. Coleridge invited a man he'd exchanged some letters with to stay at the Wordsworths: a known revolutionary named John Thelwall, who had once been arrested for treason. He had been acquitted, but he was still a radical, maybe untrustworthy, and maybe even a spy. And those "poets" were always walking about the hills, isolated from other people, and talking, talking, talking to one another. One government spy, who was actually keeping an eye on Thelwall, reported watching William and Dorothy Wordsworth following a nearby river to where it reached the sea, pulling out a notebook to scribble a few lines every so often. He thought they were plotting out a map for another French invasion. As far as William and Dorothy were concerned, they were working through some ideas for a poem.

But Wordsworth and Coleridge *were* fomenting a sort of revolution government spies wouldn't have recognized if they saw it: a literary revolution. The two poets were developing an entirely new theory of what poetry was about. Until the late 1700s, "real" poetry dealt with grand themes, it was epic, its characters were larger-than-life and spoke in the kind of flowery language one of Shakespeare's creations would immediately recognize. For the lower classes there was poetry of a sort, too: popular ballads and bawdy or silly doggerel. But that poetry wasn't considered fit to publish; it was memorized and recited on the streets or printed on pages called broadsides. Far below *any* kind of poetry came the newfangled novel.

The experiment Wordsworth had in mind—and he and Coleridge did call it an experiment, something they were testing to see if it would float—would fill the gap between roadside rhyme and high verse. Their idea was to write a set of poems whose language would echo more closely the way ordinary people talked. And the subjects would not be Greek gods or Bible stories or ancient history but ordinary people, including the poor, the homeless, the half-mad wanderers. The stress would be less on action and heroics and more on what the simple characters thought and felt. Ordinary readers would be able to relate to these people. They knew them. Perhaps they *were* them. That was something you couldn't say about the epitome of earlier English poetry, *Paradise Lost,* by John Milton, which was about God and Satan, Adam and Eve, and the loss of Eden.

All good poetry, Wordsworth wrote, "is the spontaneous overflow of powerful feelings: it takes its origin from emotion recollected in tranquillity." These new poems would speak to readers' imaginations, using rich images and precise, evocative language to paint scenes. Some would touch on the supernatural, which was Coleridge's speciality—it required a "willing suspension of disbelief." And, since Wordsworth believed people should look to poets for moral guidance, the poems would encourage good living. The result of all this philosophizing about what poetry might be was a preface, an introductory essay, to a book of poems the two men wrote entitled *Lyrical Ballads.*

Most of the twenty-three poems in the first edition of *Lyrical Ballads* were Wordsworth's; only four were Coleridge's. The two poets published the first edition of their book anonymously. As Coleridge explained, "Wordsworth's name was nothing, and mine stinks." Even if his "nothing" name wasn't connected to it right away, Wordsworth was a publisher's and printer's nightmare. His poems were never really finished. He would write a piece, then go back to it and revise it, and then revise it slightly again, sometimes right down to the moment it was ready to be printed. It was something he did all his life, which is why there are sometimes versions of Wordsworth's poems with a word or two different here and there. They're not mistakes, just different versions of work that was always in progress.

There was one poem Wordsworth wrote that he had to cram in at the last minute just as *Lyrical Ballads* was ready to be published with twenty-two poems. It was "Lines Composed a Few Miles Above Tintern Abbey," and it represented the most magical writing experience the poet had ever had. He and Dorothy were walking through Wales to catch a ferry to Bristol. They passed Tintern Abbey, the ruins of a monastery that had been left to the mercy of the elements since the time of King Henry VIII's religious reform. It was a picturesque view that inspired Wordsworth to think about Nature and mankind's place in it. For the next three days, all through the rest of the walk, he put words and lines together in his head, memorizing them as he composed—his favorite way of making up a poem. He wrote the poem down when he and Dorothy reached Bristol, and immediately sent it off to the publisher to include in *Lyrical Ballads*. For once, there wasn't a single revision.

Not everyone was comfortable when faced with poems about the sorts of people you'd avoid on the street, reading words or expressions you'd ordinarily come across in a tavern or a barnyard, not a literary society meeting. Even Dorothy, her brother's staunchest supporter, said, "I now perceive clearly that till my dear Brother is laid in his grave his writings will not produce any profit . . . however cheap his poems might be. I am sure it will be very long before they have an extensive sale." Critics weren't quite sure what to make of the poems, either; they were so different from most of what had been written before. So they gave the book a thumbs-down. Even Coleridge's old friend Southey wasn't impressed. Wordsworth's response to criticism was, "I published those poems for money and money alone." And the money wasn't bad. There were enough readers who seemed to like the poems. Sales were decent for such an unusual book. It went through four editions by 1805. Eventually, Wordsworth was even persuaded to publish the book with his name, rather than "Anonymous," attached to it.

Wordsworth thought the sales would have been better if they'd left out that spooky ancient mariner. (When he reviewed the book, Robert Southey agreed.) Late one evening in early winter, Coleridge, Wordsworth, and Dorothy had gone for a walk in the hills. They could see the sea below, whitecaps foaming and its color changing from blue through shades of gray as the sun set. Then the moon rose and spread a path of cool light on the dark, rippling water. For five months Coleridge wrote and revised, combining his impressions of the ocean with a dream about a ghost ship a neighbor had told him, and with one of Wordsworth's snippets of trivia from his voracious reading—that killing an albatross was considered bad luck by sailors. All those elements turned into Coleridge's most famous poem, a piece that let him explore his fascination with the supernatural. The original idea had been to send the poem out to magazines that printed gothic stories, just to make some money. Instead, "Rime of the Ancient Mariner" had become part of *Lyrical Ballads.*

Coleridge had a Tintern Abbey-like experience, too, but his poem didn't make it into *Lyrical Ballads.* In fact, it wouldn't be published for many years, and then it would be after the encouragement not of Wordsworth but of a very different poet. It wasn't even a complete poem. And Coleridge had little in common with his friend Wordsworth when it came to composition. Wordsworth was never finished because he kept revising. Coleridge didn't finish his poems because he lost inspiration. And sometimes the inspiration, and its loss, had to do with drugs.

One day Coleridge was out walking in the countryside, as usual. He made it as far as Lynton (about thirty miles from Nether Stowey), and was on his way home when he started feeling sick. He knocked on the door of a place called Ash Farm and was invited in to sit and rest—and take a bit of opium. Perhaps he picked up a famous seventeenth-century travelogue called *Purchas's Pilgrimage* to relax him, or perhaps he just dozed off while he was thinking about an excerpt from it, where the traveler reaches China: "Here the Khan Kubla commanded a palace to be built, and a stately garden thereunto. And thus ten miles of fertile ground were inclosed with a wall." Under the influence of the opium, he began to dream about those magical words. In his sleep, he composed

Samuel Taylor Coleridge

nearly three hundred lines of poetry about the Orient of the Khan. He remembered them clearly when he awoke three hours later, and immediately began to write them down. He'd gotten through just fifty-four lines when a visitor arrived at the farm, and he had to set his writing aside and be sociable for an hour. When the visitor left and Coleridge returned to his poem, the memory of his dream had vanished. The remaining two hundred fifty lines were lost forever.

Coleridge must have shared the fragment of a poem with William and Dorothy, since they took to calling the water container they carried on their long walks Kubla Khan, but there was no question of publishing such an incomplete—and borderline crazy—bit of verse in any edition of *Lyrical Ballads*.

Coleridge had proved himself a capable poet, but he still couldn't make a living from it. Early in 1798, he and a congregation in Shrewsbury whose church needed a minister expressed interest in each other. He was a guest preacher there one Sunday. He was always a passionate and fascinating speaker, and he impressed the congregation enough to be offered the job on January 14. Then, the very next day, he heard from the Wedgwood brothers, bankers and philosophers, the sons of the famous pottery-maker. They were willing to give him 150 pounds a year for the rest of his life, just to write poetry. It was hardly a choice for Coleridge. He had reputable patrons. He was going to be a poet.

Now that their book was launched and they were both officially poets, with funding, Coleridge and William Wordsworth, along with Dorothy, went on a trip together to Germany. The Wordsworths wanted to see the country; Coleridge wanted to study German. Coleridge picked expensive places to stay; the Wordsworths were content with humbler lodgings. Coleridge had left Sarah and his children back in England, so he was a free man, traveling alone. Dorothy was greeted with suspicion everywhere she and her brother went. The rumor spread that she was William's mistress, not his sister. Once she was even arrested for vagrancy while walking around the countryside alone, and William had to get her out of jail. The Wordsworths went back to England, but Coleridge stayed in Germany.

Back home, Coleridge's baby son Berkeley was given an inoculation against smallpox, a technique that was relatively new and not entirely understood. There were complications, and the little boy died. A friend advised Sarah not to tell her husband, as it would disturb him too much, so she bore the grief alone for months. When Coleridge finally learned that his younger son had died, he went for a long walk—but stayed in Germany. Sarah, who had to cope with the stress every day, grew more and more depressed. The Southey family took her in until she could get back on her feet. Her hair, which had been so beautiful when she was younger, began to turn dull, then fall out. She was in her mid-twenties. She looked fifty.

When they returned from Germany, the Wordsworths decided to move from the southwest of England back to their home country in the north. They found a former inn, the Dove and Olive Branch, which was now called Dove Cottage. It was in Grasmere, just a stone's throw from one of the many lakes in the area. With only six rooms, Dove Cottage was tiny compared to Alfoxden. Downstairs were the kitchen and Dorothy's bedroom. Upstairs were a living room and William's bedroom. There were also two small guest rooms; Dorothy inexplicably covered the walls of one of them with newspaper. So they wouldn't always need to use the front door for coming and going, they cut an opening from the stairway landing right into the sloping back garden. The cottage was always cramped, and it was cramped *and* cold in the winter, but the rent was only eight pounds a year.

Coleridge finally left Germany to return to England and his family. It was a quick return to real life. The Coleridge house flooded. Coleridge came down with pneumonia. His son Hartley caught some sort of skin disease that had to be treated with a foul-smelling medicine. The whole house had to be opened up and aired to get rid of the stench.

Coleridge had refused to leave what he was doing to comfort his own wife on the death of their son, but when, in the middle of all the Coleridge family mayhem, he heard that William was sick, he rushed north to be with him. It was a false alarm—but a trip that would change Coleridge's life. For the Wordsworths' old childhood friend, Mary Hutchinson, was visiting, along with her sisters Joanna and Sarah. There, at Dove Cottage, Coleridge met the love of his life. As the group "stood up round the Fire," Coleridge "pressed [Sarah Hutchinson's] hand behind her back a long time; and then Love first wounded me with a light arrow-point—poisoned, alas! and incurable."

Sarah Hutchinson was a chubby little thing, not a great beauty, although her impressive auburn-brown hair, so like Sarah Fricker Coleridge's in her younger and less stressed days, made her Esteesi's type. She was independent, a woman who could think for herself. Dorothy Wordsworth immediately sensed that she was a better match for her unstable friend than his wife could ever be—and told her so. Coleridge began writing passionately personal poetry to his new beloved. Having a wife and a lover with the same name posed a problem he had no trouble solving. He called Hutchinson Asra.

In 1802 William and Dorothy set off on an important trip to France. William had decided to marry Mary Hutchinson, and he needed to bring some sort of closure to the matter of Annette and Caroline Vallon. In her years alone, Annette had taken to calling herself "the Widow Williams." She still couldn't speak English. For Wordsworth, a "spontaneous overflow of powerful feelings" was inevitable, and he dealt with it as he always had, by writing a poem. His sonnet that begins "It is a beauteous evening, calm and free" is about his first meeting with the daughter separated from him by revolution so many years ago.

Whether it was being in love or living again in the Lake District he'd so adored as a child, Wordsworth's powerful feelings overflowed spontaneously a lot in 1802. In just one day that May he wrote three sonnets.

Dorothy, too, played a part in his writing—a larger part than she's given credit for. Someone who knew them said that the two would go "bumming and booing about, and she, Miss Dorothy, kept close behind him, and she packed up the bits as let 'em fall, and tak'em down, and put 'em on paper for him." With all the poems that have been written in the English language, it is one by William Wordsworth that appears most often in anthologies: "Daffodils." Half the credit for the poem should go to Dorothy. In her journal is an entry:

> *I never saw daffodils so beautiful they grew among the mossy stones about and about them, some rested their heads upon these stones as on a pillow for weariness and the rest tossed and reeled and danced and seemed as if they verily laughed with the wind that blew upon them over the lake, they looked so gay ever glancing ever changing.*

The images were Dorothy's, the interpretation William's, when Wordsworth created his most famous poem.

On October 4, 1802, Wordsworth married Mary Hutchinson. Dorothy was so heartbroken she refused to attend the wedding, instead staying in bed and crying. It wasn't as if the couple would be turning Dorothy out into the harsh world; she continued to live as an important part of the household for the rest of her life. The Hutchinson family refused to come to the wedding, too, but for a different reason. William, they said, was nothing but an unemployed wanderer who liked to scribble. They didn't even send a wedding present.

The following year, the newlyweds took a trip together to Scotland. They visited another up-and-coming writer, Walter Scott, who had some advice for Wordsworth. Scott was making good money. Readers were eager for the romantic adventure stories he was churning out, and he was glad to give them what they wanted. That was all it took to be a successful writer. William should try it.

A few years later Scott returned the visit by dropping in at Dove Cottage. He found his friends eating oatmeal and water for most meals and saving used tea leaves for a second soak. Scott had to sneak out after dinner and go into Grasmere to find something more appetizing and filling. Obviously, Wordsworth hadn't taken his advice.

Wordsworth and Scott were casual friends who could agree to disagree sometimes. But the bond between Wordsworth and

Coleridge was on a completely different level. Wordsworth once wrote Coleridge a letter that contained a couplet:

> *Uncertain heaven received*
> *Into the bosom of the steady lake.*

And Coleridge replied, "Had I met these lines running wild in the deserts of Arabia, I should have instantly screamed out, 'Wordsworth!'" It was incredible how well the two men knew each other, how close they really were to having one soul.

But, like most great romances, it was not fated to last.

The Poems

from LINES COMPOSED A FEW MILES ABOVE TINTERN ABBEY

by William Wordsworth

           For nature then
(The coarser pleasure of my boyish days,
And their glad animal movements all gone by)
To me was all in all.—I cannot paint
What then I was. The sounding cataract
Haunted me like a passion: the tall rock,
The mountain, and the deep and gloomy wood,
Their colors and their forms, were then to me
An appetite; a feeling and a love,
That had no need of a remoter charm,
By thought supplied, nor any interest
Unborrowed from the eye.—That time is past,
And all its aching joys are now no more,
And all its dizzy raptures. Not for this
Faint I, nor mourn nor murmur; other gifts
Have followed; for such loss, I would believe,
Abundant recompense. For I have learned
To look on nature, not as in the hour

Of thoughtless youth; but hearing oftentimes
The still, sad music of humanity,
Nor harsh nor grating, though of ample power
To chasten and subdue. And I have felt
A presence that disturbs me with the joy
Of elevated thoughts; a sense sublime
Of something far more deeply interfused,
Whose dwelling is the light of setting suns,
And the round ocean and the living air,
And the blue sky, and in the mind of man;
A motion and a spirit, that impels
All thinking things, all objects of all thought,
And rolls through all things. Therefore am I still
A lover of the meadows and the woods,
And mountains; and of all that we behold
From this green earth; of all the mighty world
Of eye, and ear,—both what they half create,
And what perceive; well pleased to recognize
In nature and the language of the sense,
The anchor of my purest thoughts, the nurse,
The guide, the guardian of my heart, and soul
Of all my moral being.

IT IS A BEAUTEOUS EVENING

by William Wordsworth

It is a beauteous evening, calm and free,
The holy time is quiet as a Nun
Breathless with adoration; the broad sun
Is sinking down in its tranquility;
The gentleness of heaven broods o'er the Sea:
Listen! the mighty Being is awake,
And doth with his eternal motion make
A sound like thunder—everlastingly.
Dear Child! dear Girl! that walkest with me here,
If thou appear untouched by solemn thought,
Thy nature is not therefore less divine:
Thou liest in Abraham's bosom all the year,
And worship'st at the Temple's inner shrine,
God being with thee when we know it not.

I Wandered Lonely as a Cloud

by William Wordsworth

I wandered lonely as a cloud
That floats on high o'er vales and hills,
When all at once I saw a crowd,
A host, of golden daffodils;
Beside the lake, beneath the trees,
Fluttering and dancing in the breeze.

Continuous as the stars that shine
And twinkle on the milky way,
They stretched in never-ending line
Along the margin of a bay:
Ten thousand saw I at a glance,
Tossing their heads in sprightly dance.

The waves beside them danced; but they
Outdid the sparkling waves in glee;
A poet could not but be gay,
In such a jocund company;
I gazed—and gazed—but little thought
What wealth the show to me had brought:

For oft, when on my couch I lie
In vacant or in pensive mood,
They flash upon that inward eye

Which is the bliss of solitude;
And then my heart with pleasure fills,
And dances with the daffodils.

KUBLA KHAN

by Samuel Taylor Coleridge

In Xanadu did Kubla Khan
A stately pleasure dome decree:
Where Alph, the sacred river, ran
Through caverns measureless to man
    Down to a sunless sea.
So twice five miles of fertile ground
With walls and towers were girdled round:
And there were gardens bright with sinuous rills,
Where blossomed many an incense-bearing tree;
And here were forests ancient as the hills,
Enfolding sunny spots of greenery.

But oh! that deep romantic chasm which slanted
Down the green hill athwart a cedarn cover!
A savage place! as holy and enchanted
As e'er beneath a waning moon was haunted
By woman wailing for her demon lover!
And from this chasm, with ceaseless turmoil seething,

As if this earth in fast thick pants were breathing,
A mighty fountain momently was forced:
Amid whose swift half-intermitted burst
Huge fragments vaulted like rebounding hail,
Or chaffy grain beneath the thresher's flail:
And 'mid these dancing rocks at once and ever
It flung up momently the sacred river.
Five miles meandering with a mazy motion
Through wood and dale the sacred river ran,
Then reached the caverns measureless to man,
And sank in tumult to a lifeless ocean:
And 'mid this tumult Kubla heard from far
Ancestral voices prophesying war!
   The shadow of the dome of pleasure
   Floated midway on the waves;
   Where was heard the mingled measure
   From the fountain and the caves.
It was a miracle of rare device,
A sunny pleasure dome with caves of ice!

   A damsel with a dulcimer
   In a vision once I saw:
   It was an Abyssinian maid,
   And on her dulcimer she played,
   Singing of Mount Abora.
Could I revive within me
Her symphony and song,

To such a deep delight 'twould win me,
That with music loud and long,
I would build that dome in air,
That sunny dome! those caves of ice!
And all who heard should see them there,
And all should cry, Beware! Beware!
His flashing eyes, his floating hair!
Weave a circle round him thrice,
And close your eyes with holy dread,
For he on honeydew hath fed,
And drunk the milk of Paradise.

Sara Coleridge

A Life in Ruins

"The Habit of My Soul"

The perfect union of poetic souls started to go sour after 1802.

Maybe it was because both Wordsworth and Coleridge were trying to grow up, trying to look like responsible, respectable family men. Very quickly, William and Mary Wordsworth filled tiny Dove Cottage with baby after baby. The cottage might have been quaint and comfortable at first, but now it was much too small. After a while the family moved to Allan Bank, a roomier home not far away. It was far from perfect; the chimneys didn't draw properly, so whenever the Wordsworths lit a fire, the house would fill with smoke.

Meanwhile, Coleridge rented a home called Greta Hall, just thirteen miles from the Wordsworths. The house had originally been built as an astronomical observatory—very appropriate for the man whose father used to take him outdoors at night to study the stars. But it was hard to pay attention to the skies when you saw the view from Greta Hall's windows of the spectacular waters and fells—the rocky, furze-covered hills of the Lake District.

Wordsworth had spent his younger years on the edge of revolutions, but he was becoming downright conservative in his middle age. With all those hungry young mouths to feed, he needed money—more money than poets made. Before too many years passed, he took on a government job. He became the man the locals went to when they needed documents stamped with an official seal. He was also getting very possessive about *Lyrical Ballads*. When a second volume was published, there was not a single poem of Coleridge's in it—not the hoary ancient mariner, not "Kubla Khan," not the haunting supernatural romance "Christabel." Coleridge sadly wrote, "As to Poetry, I have altogether abandoned it, being convinced that I never had the essentials of poetic Genius, & that I mistook a strong desire for original power." But Wordsworth wasn't writing the way he had earlier, either. Most of what he did now was a reworking of old poems. Both men admitted that perhaps they were losing their creative edge.

Maybe the division between Coleridge and Wordsworth had something to do with Coleridge's obsession with Asra Hutchinson. He had a good, patient wife. He had three children now: Hartley, Derwent, and the baby, Sara. But he couldn't get Asra out of his mind. If he heard she was staying with a relative, he'd suddenly appear in the next village over, claiming he needed to study at a library there. He launched a magazine called *The Friend,* dictating the convoluted essays he composed for its twenty-eight ponderous, unsuccessful issues to his beloved Asra, as she dutifully copied down his every word.

No one really knows how far the two took the infatuation. Maybe Asra welcomed the attention. Maybe she didn't—since a married man was practically stalking her. When Coleridge praised her beautiful hair once too often, she started wearing a cap to cover it. He asked her to spell her name without the final *h.* She kept right on spelling it the way her family always had, with the *h.* Once Dorothy Wordsworth had been supportive, but now she saw through the infatuation: "He [Coleridge] likes to have her about him as his own, as one devoted to him, but when she stood in the way of other gratifications, it was all over."

Then again, the problem between Coleridge and Wordsworth might have had to do with one of Coleridge's "other gratifications," his growing drug problem. His wife was very aware that her husband took opium—a lot of it, and every day. She could tell from his behavior when he'd just had a hit and when he was starting to feel the need for more. "Have you taken too much or too little opium?" she would ask him, as casually as if she were wondering what time it was. And cheap drugs were not for him. His preference was for a pricey variety of opium called Kendall Black Drop, downed with a glass of (probably equally pricey) brandy. For variety, he'd stir his laudanum in with a

Hartley Coleridge

refreshing drink made of quince juice flavored with cinnamon, nutmeg, cloves, and saffron.

Hartley Coleridge was old enough to know something was wrong. His parents were on the verge of breaking up; his father was a drug addict and was having an affair. So he invented a fantasy world he called Ejuxria, which he imagined he flew to on the wings of a giant bird. He could withdraw and escape there for hours at a time. When he was in the real world, he washed his hands again and again, obsessively, as many as twenty times a day. His little sister, Sara, was plagued by nightmares and slept with a lighted candle in her room.

As for Sarah, she was afraid her husband would someday use up the last of the family's money on drugs and send them all to the sort of poorhouse they'd lived near in Nether Stowey. She locked ten pounds into a desk drawer and kept it secret from Coleridge, just in case she'd need it someday to survive.

In the spring of 1803, Coleridge took out an insurance policy. If he were to die in any way except hanging, drowning, or suicide, his wife would receive a thousand pounds. He knew he was in bad shape.

That summer, Coleridge went walking in Scotland with William and Dorothy Wordsworth while the wives stayed home with the children. It was like old times again, traipsing about a wild countryside in thick-soled shoes. But the middle of a vacation may not have been the best time for Coleridge to try to go cold turkey off the drugs. He would feel too sick to walk, so the group would travel by horse cart—which was bumpy and not the most comfortable means of transportation for someone who felt nauseated.

One day Coleridge simply turned and trudged away from his friends. He wasn't wearing his walking boots, and the soles of his flimsy city shoes soon fell apart from the rough ground. While going through the agonies of opium withdrawal, with its physical symptoms of severe stomach cramps and raving nightmares racing through his fevered mind, Coleridge walked for eight days straight, a total of 250 miles. That Christmas season saw a repeat performance. He stayed with the Wordsworths, sick, until the middle of January, then suddenly walked out the door and kept going for nearly five hours and almost twenty miles.

Things were getting worse, not better. Coleridge entrusted his troubled little family back at Greta Hall to the care of that old pantisocrat Robert Southey, whose family had moved in with them after the death of a baby. Then Coleridge ran away, perhaps from his life, perhaps from himself, to the warmer climate he'd been dreaming about for some time.

He was bound for the Mediterranean. As his ship rounded the coast of Spain, it passed the Rock of Gibraltar. There was some life and curiosity left in Coleridge yet—after all, he was only thirty-one. He was one of the passengers who hopped off for a quick, touristy shore excursion, scrambling up the cliffs to see the famed colony of Barbary Apes that made their home on the Rock. Then he was on to Malta, where he worked for more than a year, writing letters for the island's governor. Next on the itinerary was Sicily—where opium poppies and hemp were grown. Everywhere he went, drugs seemed to haunt him. Then bad news reached him. There had been a death in the Wordsworth family. Coleridge would need to start for home. But it wouldn't be by the shortest route; there was still mainland Italy to see.

The man who had died was William's brother, John, a quiet man of feelings that ran as deep as the poet's own and a great favorite of everyone who knew him. He was a sea captain, though he'd always dreamed of living with his siblings in the Lake District when his sailing days were done. But in 1805, John Wordsworth's ship sank, and his was one of many lives lost. For months, Wordsworth was unable to write, and the old friend who could have comforted him was nowhere to be found.

When he got back from the Mediterranean, Coleridge finally admitted that all hope was gone for his marriage. Today it would be an obvious solution for a relationship that was plainly falling apart, but both of the Coleridges were reluctant to consider divorce as an option. In the 1800s, a divorced woman was seen as a failure. Her reputation was ruined. Her former husband would be under no obligation to provide her with any kind of support. And the Coleridge and Fricker families were no help through the crisis. Whenever the couple contacted relatives, saying they'd like to visit, the response was an emphatic no. Coleridge's siblings were afraid that Samuel and Sarah would arrive one day and Samuel would suddenly disappear the next, leaving an abandoned wife for them to care for. Coleridge wanted something better for Sarah, who was a good woman placed in a hopeless situation and the devoted mother of his children. He and Sarah finally agreed to a friendly separation. She stayed at Greta Hall with the Southeys and her daughter Sara. He was left to find his place in the world, sometimes with his two sons, who would live on and off with their father, the drug addict. Even young Sara was subjected to a tug-of-war whenever Coleridge wanted her with him at Allan Bank with the Wordsworths. Legally there was nothing her mother could do about it. That was the way custody worked back then; the father was always in the right.

For a while Coleridge tried staying with the Wordsworths, but they couldn't cope with the psychedelic merry-go-round of drugged fantasies and withdrawal agonies, either. Next he set out for London, where he hoped to find work writing and presenting a series of lectures on literature—and where he hoped to find a home and perhaps even a cure for the addiction he couldn't seem to break free from by himself. The elder Basil Montagu, who had let the Wordsworths raise his son, offered to take him in. But Wordsworth had a thing or two to say about that. He contacted Montagu and let him know just how serious Coleridge's opium addiction had become. He seems to have said that no respectable gentleman would want a person in such a shameful condition in his home, around his family, in view of neighbors and guests.

When Coleridge arrived in London, he didn't find the living arrangements he'd expected. Montagu would help, but he couldn't let the poet stay in his home. Coleridge was crushed. "Wordsworth has given me up," he wrote to his old school friend Charles Lamb. Robert Southey was livid. "Wordsworth and his sister who pride themselves upon having no selfishness, are of all human beings whom I have ever known the most intensely selfish. The one thing to which Wordsworth would sacrifice all others is his own reputation." Southey had his own drug demons. He was one of the early partakers of that "excellent air-bag," nitrous oxide, or laughing gas.

Coleridge left the Lakes for the last time in 1812. He passed right by the Wordsworths' home—and didn't stop.

Charles Lamb must have been a sympathetic listener for a man like Coleridge. In a letter to Wordsworth, he called their mutual friend "an Archangel a little damaged." Lamb was no stranger to mental crises or to habits that were difficult to break. His day job was as a drudge of a clerk. At night he caroused, and when he wasn't carousing, he wrote rather well. His sister Mary was also a talented writer—on her better days. She suffered from serious psychological problems, and Charles cared for her. The two collaborated on a retelling of stories from the plays of Shakespeare, in more modern, understandable language, especially for children. People still read that book today. But suddenly, during one of Mary's psychotic episodes, she killed their mother. Lamb managed to save her from the fate of a murderess, a life in prison, by claiming she was insane, and he managed to get her admitted to one of London's private asylums. She was fortunate her brother didn't abandon her in his grief, or she may have ended up in the dreaded "Bedlam," Bethlem Hospital for the Insane, which was the only place for charity cases to go.

At one point, the madhouse was an option Coleridge himself seriously considered. But, unlike the Lambs, he didn't have enough money to check himself into a private asylum, and even nearing rock bottom, he couldn't imagine himself in Bedlam.

It had been a long time since Coleridge had written a scrap of poetry that showed even a spark of the brilliance of his younger years. The Wedgwoods, who had supported him financially when he was an up-and-coming poet, had scaled back on their donations and finally cut him off altogether. He was a has-been. He went back to those "flycatchers," his old notebooks, and resurrected some of the projects he'd dreamed of working on years earlier, like an encyclopedia. He worked very hard at each project, for a while. Then, just like with his poem fragments, he lost interest and set each one aside, never to be completed.

For the educated middle class, respectable entertainment in the early 1800s was limited. Lecture series were popular—a little like multipart documentaries on public television or the Discovery

Channel today. Coleridge was a fountain of knowledge in all sorts of areas, and he was a powerful speaker. Lectures seemed like something he'd be good at. The talks he'd given on literature, especially Shakespeare, had been popular. But he had competition just around the corner, such as William Hazlitt, who was younger, a little more biting and incisive in style, and more lively to listen to than an obvious burnout.

Besides, Coleridge was unreliable. He'd agree to do a series of lectures, often against his doctor's advice, and would do the first couple with enthusiasm and determination. But then he'd fail to show up for one, then another—and soon the series would be canceled. And it wasn't just the lecture series. When Coleridge was invited to a social occasion, if the host wanted him to show up, he'd have to send a carriage around to knock on the door and collect him.

Coleridge's friends might have been apprehensive about getting too close to a man so bent on self-destruction, yet they were still concerned. Sometimes they had good reason. But sometimes they were so used to Coleridge's odd behavior, they automatically took a negative view. For instance, he had a habit of not showing up when he was expected, of disappearing for a while. So when, during one of those disappearances, a man's body was found in Regent's Park in London, Coleridge's friends feared the worst. Then it was announced that the dead man was wearing a shirt with the poet's name printed inside the collar. But the mourning for the creator of the ancient mariner was premature. Coleridge turned up alive and as well as he ever was at that point in his life—but missing some of the clothing he'd sent off to the laundry after a lecture.

Coleridge knew he didn't have enough strength to stay away from opium on his own, and he recognized that drugs were ruining his life. He hired a man to watch him, to keep him far away from access to opium in any form. Coleridge, however, was a genius, and his caretaker wasn't. The plan was a waste of what little spare cash Coleridge had.

Finally, in 1816, Coleridge turned to a doctor who insisted he could help him overcome his addiction, a surgeon named James Gillman. Gillman had a home in Highgate, a pleasant area on the outskirts of London; it was there he would tend to his desperate patient. Living in Highgate was almost like living out in the countryside, and it was very private. Like the man Coleridge had hired, Gillman monitored everything that came into the house for the poet under his care. Still Coleridge managed to have drugs smuggled in, stashed into packages of innocent-looking books and magazines. Setback followed setback. James Gillman had joined the long line of friends and acquaintances who had tried to help Coleridge break his devastating habit. But there was one thing Gillman did not have in common with the others. He didn't give up, despite setbacks and disappointments. He stood by Coleridge for eighteen years.

Opium addiction was not uncommon in the early 1800s, since most doctors prescribed it for just about anything. And Coleridge was not the only opium addict the Wordsworths found themselves closer to than they might have liked. Years before the problem with Coleridge reached its inevitable climax, Wordsworth had received a letter from London, written by a seventeen-year-old named Thomas De Quincey. De Quincey seemed educated and articulate, qualities Wordsworth associated with a gentleman and liked in a new friend, and he invited the boy to visit him in Grasmere sometime. What Wordsworth didn't know was that De Quincey was perhaps even more hopelessly addicted to opium than Coleridge was. Also, while the young man did live in London, it was not in the sort of fashionable comfort his letter implied. De Quincey's home turf was the filthy tenements and refuse-choked alleys of the slums, among other drug addicts and prostitutes.

It was five years before De Quincey took Wordsworth up on the offer to visit, and when the Wordsworths vacated Dove Cottage for Allan Bank, their new friend moved in, setting himself up as a tutor. It didn't take long for stories to spread that Dove Cottage's new tenant had a scandalous drug problem, and that wasn't all: He was leading what polite people would call a life of moral turpitude. When De Quincey's illiterate servant girl had a baby, he admitted it was his and married her. That was the last straw for Wordsworth; De Quincey could no longer be his friend. Wordsworth was getting more conservative the older he grew. He didn't disown De Quincey because of his deception, or because he was an opium addict, or even because he had an illegitimate child (which would have been hypocritical, considering Caroline Vallon). Wordsworth disowned him because he married a girl so far beneath him in class.

Whatever the neighbors thought, De Quincey lived at Dove Cottage for over ten years. He and the girl he'd gotten into trouble and married stayed together and had a family of eight children. And his dependence upon opium spanned more than forty years. Thomas De Quincey's claim to lasting fame was the book he wrote about his experience with drug addiction, called *Confessions of an English Opium Eater.*

As Wordsworth sank his roots deeper and deeper into the Lake District and Coleridge's life spiraled out of control, a group of younger poets came of age. They were discovering the literary theories the two old friends had formulated, then put into practice. And they were ready to test the waters of the Romantic life themselves.

The Poems

from DEJECTION: AN ODE

by Samuel Taylor Coleridge

There was a time when, though my path was rough,
   This joy within me dallied with distress,
And all misfortunes were but as the stuff
   Whence Fancy made me dreams of happiness:
For hope grew round me, like the twining vine,
And fruits, and foliage, not my own, seemed mine.
But now afflictions bow me down to earth:
Nor care I that they rob me of my mirth;
     But oh! each visitation
Suspends what nature gave me at my birth,
   My shaping spirit of Imagination.
For not to think of what I needs must feel,
   But to be still and patient, all I can;
And happly by abstruse research to steal
   From my own nature all the natural man—
   This was my sole resource, my only plan:
Till that which suits a part infects the whole,
And now is almost grown the habit of my soul.

Lord Byron

Baby Byron

"Lame Brat"

here was something in the blood of the Byrons that drew them to the dark side.

As the 1700s came to an end, the fifth Lord Byron, William, had secluded himself like a hermit in the damp, moldering walls of Newstead Abbey. The estate near Nottingham had been in the Byron family for centuries, ever since an ancestor purchased it from none other than King Henry VIII when he abolished the abbeys and monasteries. The property even included a piece of Sherwood Forest, the very real location for the famous legends of Robin Hood. The abbey and its sweeping grounds must have been magnificent in their better days. But by William's time, their better days were long gone. More and more, they were coming to resemble the dilapidation of their aging lord's soul.

As a young man, William had been wild, colorful, eccentric, full of pranks—he'd even tried to kidnap an actress who'd caught his fancy. But there is a line between the kind of eccentricity that can be excused in a lord and madness. In the end, even William Byron's title couldn't help him when he killed his cousin in the heat of an argument. Setting a precedent his grandnephew would follow in an even bigger way, William Byron was ordered never to set foot in London again as long as he lived. The man known as the Wicked Lord retreated to Newstead Abbey. The roof leaked, the walls were crumbling. The Wicked Lord let them. In the grand entryway, he laid straw and sheltered a few cows. Through the empty, winding corridors and passageways, the old man raced trained crickets.

The Wicked Lord's nephew John came dangerously close to following in his uncle's footsteps. While still a young man, he had earned the nickname Mad Jack. He was an adventurer, leaping impulsively into whatever intriguing endeavor presented itself but lacking the perseverance to stay long in any one situation. At the same time, he craved an extravagant lifestyle and was constantly in debt. His own father had disinherited him. John Byron's first wife, Lady Carmarthen, the mother of his daughter, Augusta, was dead; Augusta's maternal grandmother was raising her—as far away from the Byrons as possible. For his second wife, Mad Jack Byron chose Catherine Gordon. She was seriously overweight and had a volatile temper and a reputation for being silly and flighty, but she also had aristocratic blood, being descended from Scotland's royal Stuarts. Even better, she had inherited money, which she was glad to share with her new husband, at first.

They named their son, born on January 22, 1788, George. The baby seemed plagued by bad omens. He came into the world with a caul, a membrane, covering his face. To the superstitious, it was bad luck. Even worse, it was soon clear there was something seriously wrong with his right foot. He couldn't straighten it out; it twisted inward at the ankle.

As Jack ran through Catherine's money, she and little George moved into smaller and smaller apartments, in worse and worse parts of Aberdeen. Jack stopped living with his family. It was the only way he could stay out of prison. He was heavily in debt, and according to English law, debtors could be arrested on sight—on any day but Sunday. So he took to staying in hiding all week, venturing out only on Sundays to visit his wife and son. Then he stopped coming at all. Rumor had it he'd run away to France and become a soldier. Catherine never heard from him again and considered herself a widow.

George was a bright child, who could read by the time he was five. And, like most bright children, he was full of pranks. Once, when Catherine had visitors, he took a pillow and dressed it in some of his clothes. Then he threw it from an upstairs window, right where the shocked adults couldn't help but see. But, while he was a show-off among friends, he was painfully shy among strangers.

With a mother whose emotional instability was exacerbated by the pressing need for money to live on, young George grew up accustomed to abuse, at first of the psychological and verbal varieties. When George was old enough to start school, he had to remind his mother to send him. As time went on, his classmates laughed at her and called her a fool—and Byron couldn't deny it. "Lame brat," she called her own son, on her bad days. He blamed his clubfoot on the stylishly tight corsets she'd crammed her overweight body into, even when she was pregnant. Yet through it all he worshipped her, even remembering her as his best and only friend when she died years later.

What happened next to young George had all the trappings of a fairy tale—but a fairy tale with a dark side. A series of untimely deaths in the family left him next in line for the title of Lord Byron. Then one night in 1798, miles away from each other, ten-year-old George Gordon and his granduncle, the Wicked Lord, fell asleep—the boy in his mother's tiny flat, the old man in his bed in the sole room at Newstead Abbey whose roof didn't leak. Only one of them woke up the next morning: George Gordon, now Lord Byron, a new aristocrat.

If fairy tales came true, young Lord Byron would have lived happily ever after. Reality, unfortunately, was quite different. George and his mother set out for Newstead Abbey, a fine-sounding name for a lord's home. What they found was a dilapidated building and overgrown grounds that would cost enormous amounts of money—money they didn't have—to restore. It was a month before William Byron could be buried, because his heirs, Catherine and George, couldn't afford a funeral.

And the abuse didn't end for the young lord; it just changed.

Catherine hired a maid who took a fancy to George, with his curly auburn hair and blue eyes. Before he'd entered his teens, she had introduced him to sex. The seduction taught him a dangerous lesson very early in life—sex could be a powerful tool for amusement, for control, and for abuse. He had a hard time associating it with love; his sensitivity about his deformed foot was part of the reason. When he was a young man, handsome, muscular from swimming and exercising regularly, he met a girl he liked and who seemed to enjoy and encourage his attentions. Then he overheard his new girlfriend whispering and giggling with her friends. The stinging epithet "cripple," punctuated by her laughter, crushed his youthful ardor, replacing it with cold cynicism.

Now that they belonged to the privileged class, George's mother took him to specialists in London to see what could be done about his clubfoot. Catherine Gordon found a doctor with questionable credentials, a Dr. Lavender, who rubbed the boy's bad foot with oil, then screwed it into a rack, trying to twist it by force into the proper position. Anything that hurt so much should have worked, but it didn't. Fortunately, Catherine also took her son to a more competent doctor, who prescribed a leg brace, then orthopedic boots. But George Gordon, Lord Byron, knew he would never be perfect, no matter what the doctors did, so he often "forgot" to wear the clumsy shoes. The brace he hurled into a pond. Even as an adult, when Byron limped down a city street, boys would follow behind him, mimicking him, mocking him. He knew it, and he hated it.

It didn't help his self-image that he'd inherited his mother's weight problem. He was not quite five feet nine inches tall, but at one point he weighed more than two hundred pounds. Byron tried every fad diet of the day. He drank glasses full of sour vinegar. He chewed gum made from pine sap, hoping it would keep him from feeling hungry. He'd keep the real amount he ate a secret. In public, his associates would see him with a plate of nothing but mashed potatoes. What they didn't see was the huge dinner he'd treat himself to afterward. When all else failed, he'd binge one day, starve the next. He would lose sixty pounds, gain back that amount and more, lose the excess pounds again, and so on for all his life.

Byron loved to read, especially history and popular novels, like the youthful Coleridge's favorite, *Robinson Crusoe,* by Daniel Defoe. By the time he turned fifteen, he estimated he'd read four thousand books. The poet-in-the-making, however, denied that it was possible to read poetry for pleasure. To prepare her son for higher education, Catherine Gordon hired a tutor, the unfortunately named Dummer Rogers, an American loyalist who had fled his homeland after the Revolution. But the older Byron got, the less he cared about formal education. He was expelled from Harrow, a prep school, for excessive carousing, but was later reinstated. When the time came for him to go to university, he wanted to attend Oxford but ended up at Cambridge. As Wordsworth and Coleridge had already discovered, for young men in the early 1800s, the university years could be one long party if they wished, and Byron was never one to pass up a party. College, he said, was "the Devil, or at least his principal residence, they call it the University, but any other appellation would have suited it much better, for study is the last pursuit of the society; the Master eats, drinks, and sleeps, the Fellows drink, dispute and pun, the employments of the undergraduates you will probably conjecture without my description." One fellow partier who would remain loyal to Byron all his life was John Cam Hobhouse, who later became an influential politician.

Spooky, supernatural things and places were as popular then as they are now, so rambling old Newstead Abbey became a favorite venue for Byron's college friends. Rumors spread that its dark halls were haunted. Byron's flamboyant decorating style added to the illusion. A coffin stood at one end of the scarlet and yellow dining room, which Byron had turned into an indoor shooting gallery. Flowerpots made from the skulls of monks who had been buried at Newstead back when it had been a real abbey lined the walls. Byron also had a drinking goblet made from one of those skulls. He and his friends sometimes donned long, dark, hooded robes, like those of medieval monks, for their Newstead parties.

The handsome Byron was also establishing his reputation as a daring and dashing ladies' man. Girls, and eventually women, saw in Byron a sad, lost, searching soul they could save with their love. It was irresistible—and it was a carefully developed persona that would serve his purposes well all his life. Byron didn't want women to save him. He wanted them to provide him with a good time. During one school vacation, he and his friends planned a trip to the seaside resort of Brighton, and Byron was determined to bring along sixteen-year-old Caroline Cameron. But he knew that the inn they'd be staying at would never allow a girl to share a room with a group of college boys. Byron's unusually curvaceous, attractive "brother," "Gordon," arrived disguised in a man's breeches and a jacket, her long blond hair hidden beneath a cap.

For genuine, unconditional love, there were animals. There would always be animals in Byron's life, especially horses and dogs. As a young man, he owned two horses, Sultan and Brighton; a huge black Newfoundland, Boatswain (who died of rabies); and two bulldogs, Smut and Nelson. When he wanted to bring Smut with him to Cambridge, the school replied that students were not permitted to keep dogs in their rooms. Byron obeyed the letter of the law, but not its spirit. Until it became too difficult to confine the beast, the turret above Byron's room was home to a tame bear.

Byron could have finished his courses at Cambridge, taken the seat in Parliament's House of Lords that he was entitled to, and lived the kind of predictable life most men of his class led. But the adolescent Byron discovered poetry. The realization that his writing ability held promise so obsessed him, he took some time off from school. He read the recent works by men like William Wordsworth and Samuel Taylor Coleridge, men who had revolutionized poetry. He even went to hear one of Coleridge's lectures. This new sort of poetry was about ordinary people, talking about ordinary things and events, in language that you could hear any day on the street—but the poems were also full of genuine feeling. Byron criticized Wordsworth's poetry for sounding too much like prose, yet this new poetry did have emotion, and that was something Byron knew intimately.

Byron published his first book of poems anonymously. Some of the pieces were so nearly pornographic, he sensibly realized they would have destroyed any chance he had of someday becoming a respectable, legitimate writer. His next collection was, according to the critics, uninspired. Byron retaliated with a brilliantly derisive essay about reviewers—proving that he could indeed write.

After university, Byron did what most titled young men of his time did: He went on a long trip to Europe with a few friends. When most graduates did "the Grand Tour," they visited France and Italy, strolled through museums and attended concerts, absorbed the cream of European culture. Byron had other, far riskier plans. His Grand Tour itinerary would include Greece, Albania, Turkey—places engulfed in armed conflict. This proved too rough for most of his companions, who went back to England, leaving Byron to journey onward with his trusty servant, Fletcher (a lord could hardly be expected to rough it without a servant). As their ship crossed the Adriatic Sea and land came into view, Byron pointed to the eastern horizon with excitement and said, "That is Greece, are you content?" Fletcher wasn't as impressed as his master. "I shall not be content, my lord, until *that* is England," he answered.

Byron was far from a typical sightseeing tourist. When he arrived at the mile-wide strait called the Hellespont, he remembered the story of Leander, a man who swam across to visit his lover on the opposite shore. (This was the same story that had gotten young Samuel Taylor Coleridge a library card.) Byron was an able swimmer, and the channel offered him a challenge he couldn't resist. The single mile turned into four as the strong current carried him seaward, and it took the breast-stroking Byron over an hour to reach the other side of the strait. With his companion, a man named Ekenhead, five minutes ahead of him, he finally struggled safely ashore—and promptly wrote a poem to commemorate his accomplishment.

On another side trip outside Athens, he left some graffiti (still clearly legible today) on a pillar of the Temple of Poseidon at Cape Sounion, carving his name into the creamy marble. Despite this, he had great respect for ancient treasures. Around the time Byron was visiting Greece, his own countryman, Lord Thomas Elgin, wanted to remove carvings from the Parthenon in Athens to exhibit at the British Museum. Byron protested loudly—and to no avail—that Greece's art should stay right where it was. Ironically, on one of his voyages he shared a ship with the controversial "Elgin marbles."

In the course of his travels, Byron also exhibited a tendency to get involved in personal doings that really weren't any of his business. Eventually, it would cost him his life. During that first trip to Greece, Byron saw a noisy crowd and went to investigate the reason for the commotion. The people were carrying a large, squirming bag toward a cliff overlooking the sea; inside the bag was a young woman accused of adultery. The traditional punishment was drowning, and the crowd was about to carry out the execution. Horrified, Byron intervened and managed to talk the people into banishing the young woman from the city rather than killing her. With such persuasive powers, he might have had a career in Parliament after all.

In Greece Byron also encountered a people who touched something in his jaded, hedonistic, egotistical heart. Greece—the place where democracy had first been imagined—was under foreign rule, Turkish rule. The hills were full of guerrilla freedom fighters, making travel dangerous for pilgrims like Byron. But he appreciated what they were fighting for. It was something he'd remember through the crazy years to come. He wrote in his poem "The Isles of Greece":

> *The mountains look on Marathon—*
> *And Marathon looks on the sea;*
> *And musing there an hour alone,*
> *I dreamed that Greece might still be free. . . .*

Byron spent two years abroad, meeting rulers and bandits, enjoying rendezvous with attractive young women and equally attractive young boys, wearing flowing Turkish costumes—and writing poetry. He described his journeys and experiences in a sort of semiautobiographical travelogue in poem form, featuring a character he at first wanted to call Childe Burun, an old form of his own name. Before the poems were published, though, he changed the daring young man's name to Childe Harold. (A childe was a young nobleman.) People in England might not like to experience the actual danger of going to countries like Greece or Turkey, but they loved to read about exotic places and people in exciting situations. When Byron returned to England, he published the verses about Childe Harold, and "I awoke one morning and found myself famous."

Catherine Gordon did not live to see her son become famous—or, after a few years, infamous. She died around the time he came back from his travels abroad. Some of Byron's biographers have said that the high-strung Catherine gave herself a stroke, fuming over a bill from an upholsterer.

Although Byron didn't have to now that he was a famous poet, he still took the seat he was entitled to in Parliament as a lord. Once there, he could have lived quietly and obscurely. But causes attracted Byron's imagination, and a worthy cause soon presented itself. Lord Byron represented the city of Nottingham, not far from Newstead Abbey, where the major industry was weaving. For centuries, weavers had made a living working on hand looms in their homes. But just recently, machines had been invented that could do the work of many people much more quickly. The mechanized looms were taking away jobs, leaving workers poor and desperate. One night some men, perhaps affiliated with an antitechnology terrorist group known as the Luddites, smashed the hated machines. They were put on trial and sentenced to hang, the customary penalty for machine-breakers. This new Lord Byron was their only hope. The young lord stood up in Parliament and made a passionate speech.

I have been in some of the most oppressed provinces of Turkey, but never under the most despotic of infidel governments did I behold such squalid wretchedness as I have seen since my return in the very heart of a Christian country . . . Can you commit a whole country to their own prisons? Will you erect a gibbet in every field, and hang up men like scarecrows?

He failed. The men hanged. The factories steamed ahead.

For a nobleman, Byron always had a lot of sympathy for the common man. He caught one of his servants stealing from him. The man received the standard thief's sentence: seven years in the distant, dreaded penal colony of Australia. Byron had misgivings—his servant might never see his home and family again, which seemed a hefty price to pay for a momentary lapse of judgment. He went out of his way to obtain a royal pardon for the man and even apologized for having him arrested.

Byron soon stopped attending meetings of Parliament. There were so many fascinating distractions, primarily female. For most people, a love triangle is a difficult situation to escape gracefully. Byron being Byron, love didn't come in a triangle. It came in something closer to a pentagram.

The Poems

WRITTEN AFTER SWIMMING
FROM SESTOS TO ABYDOS

1

If, in the month of dark December,
   Leander, who was nightly wont
(What maid will not the tale remember?)
   To cross thy stream, broad Hellespont!

2

If, when the wintry tempest roared,
   He sped to Hero, nothing loath,
And thus of old thy current poured,
   Fair Venus! how I pity both!

3

For *me*, degenerate modern wretch,
   Though in the genial month of May,
My dripping limbs I faintly stretch,
   And think I've done a feat today.

4

But since he crossed the rapid tide,
   According to the doubtful story,
To woo—and—Lord knows what beside,
   And swam for Love, as I for Glory;

5

'Twere hard to say who fared the best:
  Sad mortals! thus the gods still plague you!
He lost his labor, I my jest;
  For he was drowned, and I've the ague.

Percy Bysshe Shelley

YOUNG SHELLEY

"A Demon Risen That Moment Out of the Ground"

Wordsworth was traipsing around France. Coleridge and Southey were hatching utopian schemes. Single mother Catherine Gordon was raising a four-year-old named George. And, in 1792, Timothy and Elizabeth Shelley—ages forty and twenty-nine, respectively, and a bit old to be starting a family by eighteenth-century standards—had their first child, a boy they named Percy Bysshe. Like the Gordons and the Byrons, the Shelleys came from the privileged classes. Unlike the Byrons, they were reserved, respectable people. The closest the family came to a black sheep was Timothy's father, Bysshe Shelley: he'd been born in New Jersey. But his roots were English and his sympathies were not with the rabble-rousing American freedom fighters. He returned to England, married a wealthy heiress, then another after the first died, and built himself a castle. Timothy himself was a Sussex squire who had once held a seat in Parliament.

Five sisters followed Percy—or Bysshe, as the family called him: Elizabeth, Mary, Hellen, Margaret, and another little girl who died in infancy. But Bysshe, being both the oldest and the only boy, was the spoiled favorite. And if there hadn't been an eccentric streak in the Shelley family so far, there was now. Bysshe Shelley, like Stephen King and R. L. Stine fans today, loved horror stories and the latest craze, gothic novels. From early on it was clear that he had a gift: He could make up stories even scarier and more imaginative than the ones he read. His little sisters thrilled, trembled, and probably had nightmares as their wildly creative brother told them tales of a mad alchemist who created magical potions in their attic or of the giant tortoise and snake that haunted the pond on their property. The tales were sometimes graphically punctuated by a pan of blazing coals carried through the darkened house or by sketches of devils and demons.

Most boys from the sort of respectable class the Shelleys belonged to went off to boarding school. When he turned ten, Bysshe found himself at Syon Academy, among the school's sixty boys ages eight through eighteen. After a childhood surrounded by girls, it wasn't easy for a boy like Bysshe to fit in. And he seemed like an easy target for bullies, with his fair curls, delicate features, and squeaky voice. But the other boys quickly learned that Bysshe Shelley's temper had a very short fuse, and when he was provoked—which didn't take much—he could strike out violently. More than once at mealtime, he whirled about at a boy calling him names and thrust a knife or fork through his hand right into the table. And at Syon, he also discovered more interesting potential weapons.

Shelley became fascinated with chemistry, a subject which at that time was far beyond the mathematical equations and tame solutions studied in science classes today. He continued his studies back in his room and learned things the teachers tended to omit from their lessons—such as that certain chemicals, in certain combinations, could produce incredible explosions. He was encouraged in his little experiments by one teacher whom he saw as his childhood attic alchemist come to life, a stereotypical nineteenth-century "mad" scientist and inventor—who may or may not have been aware that his young pupil was twisting chemistry toward alchemy, philosophy toward parapsychology. It didn't take long for other teachers to learn of Bysshe's fascination for things that went *boom*. During one class he was experimenting with some gunpowder and blew the top off his desk. If an unusual fire sprang up on the Syon campus, Bysshe Shelley was the most likely culprit.

From Syon, Shelley went on to Eton, a boys' preparatory school, where he found larger things to blow up. Scientists of the time were fascinated by electricity and its potential. It could kill, but some also believed it could bring the dead back to life, if only they could figure out how. An Italian named Luigi Galvani had passed an electrical current through the legs of a dead frog. They jerked and twitched as if the frog were trying to jump.

Another scientist tried a similar experiment with the head of a recently executed criminal. The man's eyes flew open and the muscles in his face contracted and relaxed. This was science right up Percy Bysshe Shelley's avenue, and he was eager to tap electricity's potential for mayhem. He literally shocked an Eton headmaster by electrifying the doorknob to his chambers. When a tree stump at the school spontaneously exploded, Shelley was ordered to send all his chemistry books back home.

Science was far from the only subject that interested young Bysshe Shelley. Spirits and the occult still fascinated him to the point where he spent hours sitting alone in the underground crypt of a church, waiting for its reputed ghost.

Meanwhile, things were happening back home for the Shelley family. Bysshe was no longer the only son. In 1806 Timothy and Elizabeth had another baby boy. On a visit home from Eton, Bysshe sat down with his baby brother, who was just learning to talk, and taught him to say "devil."

At about the same time, Shelley discovered the poetry of Samuel Taylor Coleridge and especially enjoyed "The Rime of the Ancient Mariner," which he often recited quietly to himself as he walked along. Almost prophetically, he used as a talisman some lines by Robert Southey:

> *And water shall hear me,*
> *And know thee and fly thee;*
> *And the Winds shall not touch thee*
> *When they pass by thee . . .*

Around that time, Bysshe tried his own hand at writing one of the gothic novels he so enjoyed reading. He called it *Zastrozzi*. He and his sister Elizabeth also collaborated on a similar tale with the title *Ghasta; or the Avenging Demon!!!*

From Eton, Bysshe moved on to university at Oxford, where he quickly gained a reputation for a degree of eccentricity that actually frightened many of his classmates. In some ways he was a typical college student, for then or now. His room was a mess, with clothes and books all over the floor. He slept only four hours a night, from six to ten P.M. He spent entire days reading, entire nights socializing with one of his few friends, T. J. Hogg (whom he hoped would marry his sister Elizabeth), or continuing his science experiments. His hair grew longer and longer, and his wardrobe was crammed with gaudy clothes—especially brightly striped vests. These activities were unusual, but not exactly against any university rules. But one firm Oxford requirement was daily attendance at chapel. Well-born, properly brought up young men were welcome to believe in God or not, but if they didn't, they were expected to keep the fact to themselves. Before his university days, Shelley had written letters to local clergy, portraying himself as an uneducated, curious farmhand and posing questions that got trickier and trickier as the correspondence went on, until the clergyman realized he was being set up to contradict himself. For Percy Bysshe Shelley did *not* believe in God.

Shelley's father inadvertently set the stage for what happened next. When he dropped his son off at Oxford, he stopped into the local bookshop, which also did some printing. "My son here has a literary turn," he said to the proprietor. "He is already an author, and do pray indulge him in his printing freaks." What Sir Timothy didn't anticipate was that Percy and his friend Hogg would declare themselves atheists, write a pamphlet justifying their views, and have it printed—one of the first atheist tracts ever published in England. They published it anonymously and sent out complimentary copies to Anglican bishops. For six shillings, anyone else could buy it from the Oxford bookshop. Twenty minutes after it went on display, a faculty member spotted it and reported it to the authorities. There might not have been a name on the title page, but the project smacked of Percy Bysshe Shelley. He was questioned, and on March 25, 1811, he was expelled, along with T. J. Hogg, not for *writing* the atheism pamphlet, but for refusing to admit that he'd had a part in it.

By now, Timothy Shelley suspected his oldest son was turning into a serious embarrassment to the family—and perhaps worse. Bysshe began telling friends that his father was planning to have him committed to a mental institution, which may not have been total paranoia. It was true that Squire Timothy refused to accept any mail from his son that hadn't been read first by a family attorney. He was afraid that the young man's penchant for self-expression would land the family in a trial for libel. Bysshe was understandably hurt by his family's lack of support and even announced that he wasn't interested in the Shelley inheritance, when it should come his way.

Threats of commitment to one of nineteenth-century

England's dreaded mental institutions might make some people change their ways, but Bysshe's eccentricities went on. Along the Serpentine, a waterway in Hyde Park in London, he would float toy boats, carefully folded from paper money, generally large-denomination bills. Occasionally he also set them on fire. He began an affair with a schoolteacher named Elizabeth Hitchener, nicknamed Portia, a woman considerably older than he was, with a reputation for being bold and independent. Respectable society, which required young singles to go out chaperoned, was scandalized.

Then Shelley met the Westbrook sisters, Eliza and Harriet. In Harriet he thought he'd found a kindred spirit, with her complaints that her father dominated her life and her melodramatic suicide threats. Shelley and Harriet talked about living together, but Harriet wouldn't hear of it. She insisted on a wedding, even if it was secret. In the 1800s, when lovers wanted to elope, they often ran away to Scotland, where the rules regarding marriage were less strict than in England and did not require parental permission. So one late-summer night in 1811, the two young people spent the day scurrying from coffeehouse to coffeehouse, avoiding curious eyes, until they reached an inn called the Green Dragon. When a mail coach stopped there, they slipped on and headed for Scotland with all of thirty-five pounds in Shelley's pockets. "We must live I suppose on love," Shelley wrote to T. J. Hogg. Percy Bysshe Shelley and Harriet Westbrook were married on August 28, 1811.

Shelley may have declared that he wasn't interested in an

inheritance, but when his father finally tracked the young couple down and cut off Percy's allowance, the newlywed husband mailed off an abusive letter. Timothy was actually afraid that his son would break into the home and attack his own family.

Shelley claimed to disdain the rich, but he and Harriet copied their lifestyle. They rented comfortable lodgings, bought extravagant clothes and furnishings—then disappeared when the time came to pay their bills. And before the invention of telephone directories or Internet searches, it was not that easy to track down someone who didn't want to be found.

Before long, T. J. Hogg joined the young couple in Scotland. Then Shelley, always suspicious to the point of paranoia, got the idea that his friend was romantically interested in Harriet. The young couple took off very suddenly for a trip to the Lake District. Hogg walked into the house one day to find empty cupboards, a note from the newlyweds—putting him on the wrong trail should he consider following them—and a bill from the landlord.

Shelley had heard about the poets and writers who made their home in the Lake District—Wordsworth, Coleridge, Southey, De Quincey. But in the four months he spent in Chestnut Cottage at Keswick, the only one he actually met was Southey, who assured Shelley that he'd eventually outgrow all his silly ideas. Wordsworth was away on business. The only one who later regretted having missed him was Coleridge, who had been presenting a lecture series in London. They missed each other by just two weeks. Coleridge had heard of the wild track the young man's life was taking and felt he might have saved him from much heartache. Even De Quincey, the self-professed drug addict, described Shelley as "such a lunatic angel, such a ruined man." The townspeople of Keswick certainly weren't unhappy when the Shelleys announced they would be leaving. Percy was still conducting his experiments with electricity and explosions, and his landlord was constantly receiving complaints about noises and peculiar lights in the night sky.

From the Lake District, the Shelleys moved on to Dublin, Ireland. Shelley fancied himself a political radical, and he turned his writing talents to putting out pamphlets encouraging the Irish to rise up against English oppression and rely on education to overcome their legacy of poverty. He did little but attract attention to himself and gain a loyal teenage servant, Dan Healy. When the Irish prime minister Spencer Perceval was assassinated, Shelley's subversive pamphlets aroused suspicion, but because at nineteen he was still a minor, he could not be formally investigated. The Shelleys moved back to England, to the pleasant seaside village of Lynmouth. Many of the towns on England's southern coast feature towering cliffs overlooking the sea. The house and lush garden the Shelleys rented was on just such a cliff, and could only be reached on foot by way of a steep, narrow path.

Shelley was still fancying himself a radical, but this idea had taken a sexual turn. Marrying Harriet Westbrook hadn't made him forget his Portia, Elizabeth Hitchener. She joined the young couple's household in Lynmouth and started calling herself Bessie. The neighbors assumed she was a servant. When Harriet's sister, Eliza, heard about the odd living arrangements, she convinced Harriet to put her foot down and demand that her precious Percy send his ex-girlfriend packing. Elizabeth Hitchener returned to her home haunted by the gossip that she had been the live-in mistress of a married man. It took some time before she was again considered respectable enough to be a teacher. It says something about her determination and strength of character that she eventually succeeded.

Percy Bysshe Shelley couldn't help calling attention to himself. In London he'd floated paper-money boats on the Serpentine. In Lynmouth he amused himself by taking inflated pigs' bladders down to the seashore and setting them asail. Then he discovered something even more flamboyant. If he lit a fire beneath a small piece of silk, he could create a miniature hot-air balloon. Sometimes they flew; sometimes they caught fire. Sometimes they did both, and flaming balloons could be seen drifting from the cliffs around the Shelley's house. Occasionally Shelley sent off his balloons with one of his subversive pamphlets attached, but other times he did it just for fun, especially on his and Harriet's birthdays, which were just three days apart.

So far, the underage Shelley had escaped jail for his radical leanings, but his servant, Dan Healy, wasn't so lucky. One day when he was pasting Shelley's radical posters around town, he was caught by the police and put in prison. Shelley had enough money to pay the jailers to give Dan special treatment but not enough to bail him out. With the police so close to cornering their real radical, the Shelleys pulled up stakes in Lynmouth and moved on, this time to a cottage called Tan-yr-Allt, in Tremadoc, Wales. Around this time, Shelley reconciled with T. J. Hogg, who wrote of seeing his old friend again, "Bysshe looked, as he always looked, wild, intellectual, unearthly; like a spirit that had just descended from the sky; like a demon risen that moment out of the ground."

Once again, the Shelleys attracted negative attention. In 1814, in the English city of York, a group of workers at a woolens factory were executed because they were suspected of being Luddites—the same sort of disenfranchised group Byron had defended in Parliament. Shelley suggested taking up a collection to help the men's families.

Dan Healy had gotten out of jail by then and returned to his master, and word spread through the little Welsh village that the Shelleys were harboring an ex-con. Shelley, always on the verge of paranoia, would go to bed with loaded pistols, afraid that someone might break in and attack him and Harriet. Being paranoid doesn't necessarily mean someone's not out to get you. On the night of Friday, February 26, shots rang out, Tan-yr-Allt's windows were broken, and its lawn was ruined. Shelley insisted someone had tried to assassinate him, and he had a bullet hole in his nightshirt to prove it. Someone, according to Shelley, was trying to stop him from writing. And so, once again, the Shelleys were in search of a new place to live. Harriet was especially concerned. She was expecting their first child.

Shelley *was* doing some groundbreaking writing just around the time of the mysterious attack. He was preparing for the publication of a poem called "Queen Mab," which was packed full of fairly radical ideas: atheism, free love, the overthrow of kings in favor of the common folk, even vegetarianism. (Don't forget, an English breakfast was heavy on sausage, bacon, and kippers, and dinners were built around boiled beef and mutton. Shelley's personal diet plan—and he did record every bite in a journal—was based more on nuts, raisins, bread, honey, and tea, of course.) Just to make sure readers understood the points he was making in his allegorical way, Shelley annotated his poem extensively.

His hopes for "Queen Mab" lay not in financial reward, but in the satisfaction of getting his message into print and into readers' hands. "I expect no success," he wrote to his printer. "Let only 250 copies be printed. A small neat Quarto, on fine paper & so as to catch the aristocrats: They will not read it, but their sons and daughters may." Shelley was right. The attractive, authorized version of the poem was not a best seller. But the radical rabble discovered it, and bootleg copies were soon circulating in the back alleys of London, Edinburgh, Manchester, and other industrialized cities.

With the birth of his daughter, Shelley had what he saw as a prime opportunity to put into practice the things he was preaching. The famous philosopher Jean-Jacques Rousseau advocated raising children like animals, wild and free—as Wordsworth had tried raising Basil Montagu. The idea sounded perfect to Shelley. With Harriet it was a different story. She went along with naming the blond, blue-eyed girl Ianthe, after a character in "Queen

Mab." But when it came to breast-feeding the child indefinitely and allowing her to run naked everywhere they went, she drew the line.

Harriet might also have had quite an opinion to offer if she'd known that her young husband, just turned twenty-one, had another hands-on test of one of his radical ideas up his sleeve. He was partial to the freethinking, far-ahead-of-its-time philosophy of an English writer named William Godwin. Or perhaps he was just partial to Godwin's teenage daughter, Mary.

The Poems

To Wordsworth

Poet of Nature, thou hast wept to know
That things depart which never may return:
Childhood and youth, friendship and love's first glow,
Have fled like sweet dreams, leaving thee to mourn.
These common woes I feel. One loss is mine
Which thou too feel'st, yet I alone deplore.
Thou wert as a lone star, whose light did shine
On some frail bark in winter's midnight roar:
Thou hast like to a rock-built refuge stood
Above the blind and battling multitude:
In honoured poverty thy voice did weave
Songs consecrate to truth and liberty,—
Deserting these, thou leavest me to grieve,
Thus having been, that thou shouldst cease to be.

A Song: "Men of England"

Men of England, wherefore plough
For the lords who lay ye low?
Wherefore weave with toil and care
The rich robes your tyrants wear?

Wherefore feed and clothe and save
From the cradle to the grave
Those ungrateful drones who would
Drain your sweat—nay, drink your blood?

Wherefore, Bees of England, forge
Many a weapon, chain, and scourge,
That these stingless drones may spoil
The forced produce of your toil?

Have ye leisure, comfort, calm,
Shelter, food, love's gentle balm?
Or what is it ye buy so dear
With your pain and with your fear?

The seed ye sow, another reaps;
The wealth ye find, another keeps;
The robes ye weave, another wears;
The arms ye forge, another bears.

Sow seed—but let no tyrant reap:
Find wealth—let no impostor heap:
Weave robes—let not the idle wear:
Forge arms—in your defence to bear.

Shrink to your cellars, holes, and cells—
In halls ye deck another dwells.
Why shake the chains ye wrought? when see
The steel ye tempered glance on ye.

With plough and spade and hoe and loom
Trace your grave and build your tomb
And weave your winding-sheet—till fair
England be your Sepulchre.

Mary Godwin

MARY GODWIN

"Let Thy Love in Kisses Rain"

*B*lended families are not an invention of the twenti-
eth and twenty-first centuries. Mary Godwin was the product of
one of the most confusing blended families in history, and she
was born in 1797.

At the center of the family was William Godwin, a publisher
and bookseller. This may sound like an innocuous occupation,
but that depended on the kind of books one published and sold.
In his youth, Godwin had been an author as well—of the latest
fad, novels. His early works were far less literary and philosophical than those he would eventually become known for. They
were pre-Harlequin, bodice-ripping romances, the sort of book
one bishop claimed was responsible for a sudden rise in the num-
ber of prostitutes, homosexuals, and earthquakes.

Revolution was in the air by the late 1700s, and Godwin supported both the American uprising against his own country and the French revolt against their tyrant king. He even managed to get his hands on the key to the infamous Paris prison, the Bastille, which was liberated right at the beginning of the French Revolution. He sent the key to George Washington as a symbol of liberty. Among Godwin's friends and followers were writers and poets who shared his views on mankind's inalienable right to freedom, including Coleridge and Wordsworth.

Bookshops in the late 1700s and early 1800s were something like Borders and Barnes & Noble stores today. They didn't sell just books. They were places where avid readers congregated, sat in comfortable nooks, and held long conversations about what they were reading. Bookshops were often also associated with a particular publisher, as William Godwin's was. Godwin believed that books, and especially novels, were an ideal way to instruct the less educated fairly painlessly. Unfortunately, his own works were on the wordy side, abstract and full of complicated ideas, and not great favorites of the audience he was aiming at. But sometimes as a publisher he hit a winner, like *The Swiss Family Robinson*, by Johann David Wyss.

William Godwin also believed in what was known at the time as "free love," the idea that if two people loved each other they should be able to live together, married or not. In fact, Godwin was opposed to the whole idea of marriage. But then he met Mary Wollstonecraft.

Mary was born to a working-class family. The best most

women with her background could hope for in life was to become a maid in the home of a wealthy family. But she was smart and ambitious. She learned to read German and French. With these abilities, she became a translator. Like Wordsworth, she was a young activist around the time of the French Revolution. Unlike Wordsworth, she actually understood the French language; she followed the issues and was sympathetic to the cause of freedom—not just freedom for the French common people, but also for women. She stated her beliefs in *A Vindication of the Rights of Women,* one of the first genuine feminist manifestos ever written.

She may have claimed that women didn't need men to be fulfilled and successful, but her life told a different story. First she had a relationship with a Swiss artist named Henry Fuseli. Next she lived in France with Gilbert Imlay. Part of her fascination with him might have been that he was American and had actually fought in the American Revolution. Mary and Imlay had a daughter, named Fanny, in their time together. But the "free" part of free love meant that both parties were free to explore other relationships. Imlay became involved with another woman. Mary refused to believe her affair with Imlay was truly over. She proposed moving in with the new couple. Imlay didn't think that was a good idea. Mary attempted suicide.

Back in England, Mary and her young daughter found themselves living just down the road from an old acquaintance of Mary's, William Godwin. It was inevitable that two people with such similar views of life would strike up a friendship, even fall in love—and then, though both opposed the very idea of it, would get married. But marry they did. They had a child together, a girl they named Mary. At the time, one out of every ten pregnant women died as a result of childbirth. Just days after Mary Godwin's birth, the medical complications that all too often killed new mothers claimed Mary Wollstonecraft's life.

Suddenly, William Godwin, the antimarriage philosopher, was a widower with two very young children to raise—one just a newborn baby. One of his neighbors was a widow, Mary Jane Clairmont, with two children of her own. She quickly and conveniently became the next Mrs. Godwin and bore her new husband a son, William. So eventually the confusingly blended Godwin household was made up of Fanny, the child of William Sr.'s former wife and another man; Mary, Godwin's daughter with his first wife; William, his son with his second wife; and the second wife's two children from her previous marriage, Jane and Charles.

The Godwin family was a prime candidate for all sorts of neuroses. While the children were young (and, presumably, running around the house engaged in arguments that undoubtedly contained the words "you're not my *real* sister/brother/mother/father" and generally disproving many of his carefully crafted philosophical theories), Godwin himself was often ill. Vegetarian diets were all the rage with philosophers and health fanatics, so he had cut down on the amount of meat he ate. Today there are vitamin supplements to make up for any dietary deficiencies.

Back then, there weren't. Becoming a vegetarian was not a prescription for good health in the early nineteenth century.

Godwin was also critical of the way other people raised their children, even if they were being raised as he advocated. The Coleridges sometimes visited the Godwins early in their marriage, bringing along little Hartley. In fact, when Hartley was three he announced that when they grew up, Mary Godwin—who was one year old at the time—was going to be his wife. He also once whacked "Mr. Gobwin" on the leg with a bowling pin. After a few run-ins with Hartley, Godwin sat down with Sarah Coleridge for a long talk about the proper way to bring up a child. She certainly didn't see *his* youngsters running wild the way Hartley did, now did she?

Or . . . did she?

Fanny Godwin was the favorite of her father-in-law (stepparents were called in-laws in nineteenth-century England), probably simply because she caused the least trouble. She may have been the daughter of two revolutionary spirits, but she herself was a quiet, plain young woman who enjoyed working around the house like a good girl of the times. Fanny's half-sister Mary was the prettier of the two—and, her father admitted, much harder to handle. When she got upset she developed some sort of problem with her arm; some accounts say it grew weak, others that it broke out in a kind of dermatitis or eczema. She'd be sent away to the country or the seaside for a vacation, where she'd quickly begin feeling better—until she arrived home. The

Godwin household just didn't agree with her. Jane Clairmont was a year younger than Mary, and as adolescents they became little partners in crime.

Eight years after Hartley Coleridge had proposed to Mary Godwin, his father was again a visitor in the Godwins' parlor. This time the circumstances were very different. The poet's marriage had failed, he was battling the demon of drug addiction and losing, his creative brilliance was a thing of the past. But he still had the poems he'd written in better times, and a mesmerizing voice to recite them with. That Sunday evening, the poet sat down among the Godwin adults to recite "The Rime of the Ancient Mariner." It was late, and Mary and Jane were supposed to be asleep in bed. Instead, they were hiding behind the parlor sofa while the bearlike man with the wild hair and enthralling voice told the riveting story of a cursed ship—until he noticed two girls peeking at him. Godwin was about to punish them, but Coleridge invited them to stay and listen. In just a few more years, Mary would publish her own poem, thanks to her father; she had an affection for poets and an ear for good verse. As it turned out, she would need both.

A man with a philosophy like William Godwin's naturally attracted most of England's freethinkers, so it was inevitable that Percy Shelley would eventually fall under his influence. The two men met in 1812. Godwin didn't think much of his new young friend's views on poetry, and perhaps on life in general. "You love a perpetual sparkle and glittering," he stated accusingly. Before long Shelley's real attraction to the Godwin house was not the philosopher or the cerebral conversation. It was that dark, pretty, smart daughter of his.

In 1814 Mary Godwin, age seventeen, stood at her mother's grave, swearing her undying love for Percy Bysshe Shelley. Harriet was still very much married to him. In fact, she was pregnant again when she received a letter from her husband, informing her that he was in love, just not with her at the moment. Harriet packed up and went to stay with her father. William Godwin wasn't thrilled, either. Free love was a provocative concept—just not when it involved one's own teenage daughter and a married man with a family.

What happened next took place on "a dark and stormy" night, like something out of one of Shelley's beloved gothic novels. On July 28, 1814, with thunder rolling and lightning flashing, Shelley arrived at Godwin's house to find two teenage girls waiting: Mary Godwin and Jane Clairmont. They fled London and raced their carriage to the coast to find a boat ready to take them to France. Once again, Shelley was eloping with a woman he loved. Harriet was still his wife, raising his children and about to bear him another one. But he'd fallen in love with Mary Godwin, and nothing would keep them apart. Jane came along just to get away from the Godwin household.

Waves crashed into the small boat as it crossed the English Channel, and Mary was ill by the time the sun finally rose and the group saw Calais, France, before them in the dawn. Her problem may have been seasickness. Or it may have been morning sickness.

And, thanks to a faster boat, there in Calais was a frantic Mrs. Godwin, demanding that the girls—or at least her own daughter, Jane—come home with her. Both refused.

The escape hadn't been very well planned. By the time they reached Paris, they had no money; Shelley had to sell his watch. Only Jane spoke enough French to get by. Slowly they began walking through France with the goal of reaching Lake Lucerne in Switzerland. They survived on bread and milk, love, and the poetry of England's newest literary sensation, Lord Byron. Like some sort of nature god frolicking with his nymphs, Shelley splashed naked in the streams they passed while the girls sat by and admired. Somewhere along the road, he thought to write another letter to Harriet, inviting her to join them, since they were all having such a good time.

The trio finally returned to England when what little money they had scraped together ran out. Shelley was still hoping Harriet would agree to a life together with him and Mary. And he hoped she would help him out financially, since he was broke. Harriet had her baby in November. Mary's came three months later, but the girl died within days.

As if the Godwin family weren't already dysfunctional enough, Jane Clairmont began striking out on her own. She wanted to be an actress or maybe a novelist, she said, as she changed her name to Claire. She was a small, solidly built young woman with dark hair, not exactly beautiful, and certainly not as bright as Mary, but determined and with a decent voice for the stage. The casting couch isn't a Hollywood invention; it existed in London in the 1800s, and Claire Clairmont wasn't above climbing onto it if that's what it took to get what she wanted. At first what she wanted might really have been to be on stage. But there was a dark, attractive, brooding, charismatic manager at London's famous Drury Lane Theatre. He was an acquaintance of her father's. In fact, Coleridge himself had introduced the two men after one of his lectures. Like Mary's lover, he was a famous poet (although Godwin criticized his work, saying, "All his poems are the same poem with a different title"). There was a whiff of scandal about him, but after that mad dash to France with her stepsister and her married lover, Claire was no stranger to scandal. The theater manager was married, but that minor complication hadn't deterred Mary. Claire's chosen man even had a title—he was a lord.

The Poems

THE INDIAN GIRL'S SONG

by Percy Bysshe Shelley

I arise from dreams of thee
In the first sleep of night—
The winds are breathing low
And the stars are burning bright.
I arise from dreams of thee—
And a spirit in my feet
Has borne me—Who knows how?
To thy chamber window, sweet!—

The wandering airs they faint
On the dark silent stream—
The champak odours fail
Like sweet thoughts in a dream;
The nightingale's complaint—
It dies upon her heart—
As I must die on thine
O beloved as thou art!

O lift me from the grass!
I die, I faint, I fail!
Let thy love in kisses rain
On my lips and eyelids pale.
My cheek is cold and white, alas!
My heart beats loud and fast.
Oh press it close to thine again
Where it will break at last.

Lord Byron

Byronic Entanglements
"Mad, Bad, and Dangerous to Know"

Four women drove George Gordon, Lord Byron, from England forever: an obsessive playgirl, a naïve wife, a strange estranged sister, and an aspiring actress.

At twenty-seven, Lady Caroline Lamb was married and well-connected. Her husband, William, Lord Melbourne, would later become Queen Victoria's first prime minister. But she had a wild spirit—one of her youthful nicknames had been Young Savage—and marriage had done little to tame her. In an age when women grew their hair long and luxurious and wore elaborate dresses, Caro Lamb cropped her blond hair as short as a boy's and enjoyed dressing in trousers. The Young Savage also had a roving eye for men. When she came across Lord Byron's poetry, she was determined to meet the man who'd written those provocative verses. They were introduced at a dinner. She pronounced him "mad, bad, and dangerous to know" and turned her back on him. She was, of course, inviting him to pursue her. And, of course, he did. He sent her a carnation and a rose. When Caroline Lamb died sixteen years later, these flowers, carefully dried and preserved, were found in her room.

Their entanglement started out as a mutual flirtation. They moved in the same social circles—though if Byron happened to be at a party Caro wasn't invited to, he would often find her waiting for him outside, with the coachmen and horses, sometimes disguised as a page boy. Maybe it was just a rumor, maybe it had a shred of truth, but a story spread that Caro was once delivered to Lord Byron's place at a dining room table on a silver serving tray. Beneath the tray's cover, she lay stark naked. For Caro, the most irresistibly sexy thing about Byron was his "underlook," the way he'd turn those inscrutable dark blue eyes up at a potential conquest from beneath his long, thick lashes.

The attraction was mutual. Byron wrote to Caroline:

> Your heart, my poor Caro (what a little volcano!) pours lava through your veins. . . . I have always thought you the cleverest, most agreeable, absurd, amiable, perplexing, dangerous, fascinating little being that lives now.

The affair with Caro Lamb gave Byron excitement and passion, but he found himself needing more—not true love, but money. He was not only a lord, he was an extravagant lord, with an expensive lifestyle. White linen trousers were his signature outfit. Unfortunately, in those days before dry cleaning and washable linens, they were constantly getting dirty and were nearly impossible to clean, and so he wore each pair only once. He ordered them from his tailor in batches, two dozen at a time.

He could have made a comfortable living from his hugely popular poems, but he refused to accept payment for them; as a lord, it would have been beneath him. In fact, when Coleridge was desperately in need of money, Byron even tried to get his publisher to transfer his royalties to his fellow poet. He was hoping to sell Newstead Abbey, which *was* an acceptable way for a lord to make money, but in its dilapidated condition it wasn't exactly prime real estate. The only way out of his financial troubles, as Byron saw it, was to follow in the footsteps of his father and marry an heiress. And, conveniently, Caro Lamb had led him to just the girl.

Caro's mother-in-law, Lady Melbourne, had a twenty-year-old niece, Anne Isabella Milbanke—Annabella. Annabella was Caro's opposite: a plump, serious, dark-haired innocent with a passion for Jane Austen's novels and, of all things, mathematics. Perhaps most attractive to Byron (after the money she would eventually inherit, of course) was the fact that she did not dance. A new fad, the waltz, was all the rage, and Caro drew perverse delight in dancing while Byron, self-conscious of his deformed foot, could only watch. Although he admitted, "I should like her more if she were less perfect," Byron asked Lady Melbourne to inquire whether Annabella would consider him as a suitor. The scholarly Miss Milbanke promptly turned Byron's offer down. Byron wrote to Lady Melbourne, "I thank you again for your efforts with my Princess of Parallelograms. . . . We are two parallel lines prolonged to infinity side by side, but never to meet." But there is another sort of geometry in which parallel lines *can* intersect, and it would soon be working its mathematical magic for Byron and Annabella.

The third woman in Byron's romantic pentagram was Augusta Leigh, his half-sister. Catherine Gordon had arranged for her son to meet Augusta when he was seventeen and she was twenty—and Augusta's protective grandmother, who had kept her away from the Byrons all her life, was dead. The old woman had been wise. Before long, Augusta was calling her younger brother Baby Byron; to the poet, his sister was Gus or Goose. Augusta married Colonel George Leigh, had three daughters, and moved to Cambridge, but grew closer and closer to her brother. Augusta was a grown woman, a mother, but she carried on conversations with her brother in a peculiar sort of baby talk he called her "crinkum-crankum." Rumors flew that the relationship between Lord Byron and his sister was a little more than "close," especially after Augusta's daughter Elizabeth Medora was born in 1814 and the busybodies who counted off the months couldn't quite get the timing to work in George Leigh's favor. For her part, Medora would always claim Lord Byron as her father.

Nothing calms down a scandal like the appearance of respectability. Byron renewed his pursuit of Annabella Milbanke.

Lady Caroline Lamb

When he proposed a second time, again through Lady Melbourne, the Princess of Parallelograms was persuaded. Whatever was happening between Byron and his sister, they were being discreet enough for it to continue, if they wanted it to, even if he married. Caroline Lamb, however, was another story.

What had begun as a flirtation turned into an obsession for Caro. Byron wrote her a letter to tell her that their six-month relationship had to come to an end. After reading the news, Caro grabbed a razor, threatening to kill herself. She only let go when her mother tried to get the razor away from her and looked likely to get hurt herself. Caro wrote back to Byron, "You have told me how foreign women revenge; I will show you how an Englishwoman can."

More than once, at social occasions both Caro and Byron were attending, Caro approached her former lover with a dinner knife clutched in her hand. One time she threatened to stab herself. Melodramatically, Byron said, "Do, my dear. But . . . mind which way you strike with your knife—be it at your own heart, not mine—you have struck there already." Pressing the knife into her palm, she drew blood.

On another occasion, she aimed her knife at Byron's hand. At the last moment, she hesitated. "I mean to use this," she whispered.

"Against me, I presume," he replied nonchalantly. Caro's hand sank to her side.

There were other incidents, with broken glass, with scissors.

When physical violence, self-mutilation, and suicide threats wouldn't convince Byron of her undying love, Caro threw herself at him—literally. She ran away into the night dressed as a boy, her husband's father calling into the street that her lover had had enough of her. She arrived at Byron's door and refused to leave. The poet's faithful friend John Hobhouse had to pick her up and carry her away, squirming and screaming. Caro sold her jewelry and ran away again, this time to the docks, intending to book passage on a ship, any ship, no matter where it was going. Byron managed to track her down and return her to her mother, who promptly suffered a stroke. One day Byron opened an envelope and discovered a lock of curly blond hair—obviously cut from a part of the body other than the head—and a note from "Your Wild Antelope."

Unrequited love soon turned to bitterness. Her husband was the master of a large estate bordering a farming village. One night Caro asked the local people to build a huge bonfire. In the middle of an eerie ceremony, flames and smoke rising high into the sky, an effigy of Lord Byron was thrown onto the pyre and burned to ashes. Meanwhile, back at the Lamb home, the servants were busy sewing new metal buttons onto their uniforms. Embossed on the buttons were the words *Ne crede Biron*— "Don't trust Byron." The phrase was a mocking parody of the Byron motto, *Crede Byron*. Caro then set a literary goal of her own: she would write a steamy novel. The names may have been changed to protect the not-so-innocent, but the book was clearly about her affair with Byron and their messy breakup.

Ever the stalker, Caro left one last memento in Byron's copy of a popular gothic novel called *Vathek*, something far less disturbing than most of her mementos—the simple words "Remember me." After finding the note, Byron wrote:

Remember thee! remember thee!
Till Lethe quench life's burning streams
Remorse of shame shall cling to thee
And haunt thee like a feverish dream.

Remember thee! Ay, doubt it not,
Thy husband too shall think of thee,
By neither shalt thou be forgot,
Thou false to him, thou fiend to me.

In spite of Caroline Lamb's scenes and the rumors surrounding Augusta Leigh, and beset by one postponement after another, Lord Byron and Annabella Milbanke were married the day after New Year's Day, 1815. Almost immediately, Annabella must have suspected that happily ever after was not in the cards. As the couple rode away from the ceremony, the new husband was singing a song he'd picked up on his travels to the East—not a joyful wedding song, but a funeral dirge from Albania. Later he would tell friends that, on his wedding night, he awoke to see the drapes surrounding the bed weirdly lit by flickering red candle-light. "Good God, I am surely in hell," was his reaction. Among the love letters Byron sent his bride is one with the ironic sentiment "I have great hopes that we shall love each other all our lives as much as if we had never married at all." But it was not complete unhappiness. Byron wrote one of his most beautiful love poems, "She Walks in Beauty," on his honeymoon, setting it to the tune of one of composer Isaac Nathan's "Hebrew Melodies." The newlyweds affectionately called each other Pip-pin (Byron's nickname for his young wife) and Dear Duck (hers for him).

Giving Byron the benefit of the doubt isn't easy, but to be fair, Annabella wasn't exactly prepared for marriage. When her new husband explained that they would need to economize, she agreed to find ways to save money—such as making do with just one house and one carriage, far less than most young couples in their social position owned. And she had led a very sheltered life.

She probably knew next to nothing about sex. She was not exactly the partner Byron, whose conquests included live wires like Caro Lamb, perhaps his own half-sister, and assorted young men, was accustomed to.

Byron's private idiosyncrasies quickly surfaced. He disliked watching women eat and would not join his wife at the

Lady Byron

dinner table. He'd discovered fad diets and bulimia to control his weight. He began collecting exotic animals, starting with a macaw and a parrot. He kept loaded guns throughout Newstead Abbey. Most disturbing, he flew into screaming rages at the slightest provocation. The servants began to fear for their new young mistress's life and secretly made certain that Annabella was never alone.

The wedding ring Byron gave his wife had originally been his mother's. Catherine Gordon had been a large woman, much larger than tiny Annabella, so, in those days before ring sizing was an option, she tied a length of black ribbon around it to make it fit better, which her new husband considered an unlucky omen. One evening, when Byron exploded into one of his rages, Annabella pulled the ring off—and it flew across the room and into the fireplace. That didn't exactly calm Byron down.

The marriage was doomed from the start, but it went downhill when Byron invited a long-term houseguest to stay with him and his new wife: his sister Augusta. (Her children were also invited, but Byron wasn't wild about babies. He suggested that his nieces and nephews be confined to cages during the visit.) Annabella might have been sheltered and naïve, but even she knew that something wasn't right in the relationships at Newstead, especially when Byron wrote up his will and left almost everything to his sister and her children. But in the 1800s, it was a wife's duty to submit to her husband's every desire and bear her husband's children.

Less than three months after the wedding, Annabella announced that she was pregnant. Throughout the pregnancy, Byron grew more and more violent and unstable. He even pointed one of his loaded pistols at Annabella. When she went into labor, the expectant father expressed a hope that both mother and child would die.

Annabella gave birth to a daughter, Augusta Ada, on December 10, 1815. Almost exactly one month later, in the middle of the night—and after just a year of marriage—Annabella and the baby fled Newstead Abbey. At first her parents thought it was just a misunderstanding that would be quickly patched up, but as Annabella described the scenes and abuse she'd endured, they agreed that they could not send their daughter and her baby back to such perversion. A legal separation was the only solution. Divorce was out of the question. In England in the early 1800s, it took an Act of Parliament, literally, to be granted a divorce, and only a man could request one. Annabella was also afraid that Byron would get custody of little Ada (there was no way Annabella would call her daughter by Byron's sister's name!). In those days, the law was on the side of the father unless he could be proven an unfit parent. Fortunately for Annabella, there was plenty of dirt to be had on Byron—and Caroline Lamb gladly provided her with much of it. In April, Annabella was granted a legal separation from Lord Byron on the grounds of adultery, life-threatening cruelty, incest, and homosexuality. He never again saw his wife or his baby daughter Ada.

Despite the domestic drama that was Byron's life, he managed to find opportunities to write. In fact, the more conflict he experienced, the more he found to write about: "All convulsions end with me in rhyme." In the midst of the rumors of incest between him and Augusta, for instance, he was writing a poem called "The Bride of Abydos," about cousins in love. He was the sort of poet who could dash off clever rhymes and phrases quickly and easily—he finished *The Corsair,* which the composer Giuseppe Verdi later turned into an opera, in just ten days. And that dashed-off story-poem was a hit, selling over ten thousand copies the day it hit the booksellers' shelves. Wordsworth had called poetry "a spontaneous overflow of emotion," and for Lord Byron, that was exactly what writing was. "I can never get people to understand that poetry is the expression of excited passion, and that there is no such thing as a life of passion any more than a continuous earthquake, or an eternal fever. Besides, who would ever shave themselves in such a state?" Grinding out poetry was "a torture, which I must get rid of, but never . . . a pleasure. On the contrary, I think composition a great pain."

But Byron's long narrative poems, full of adventure and often featuring the Middle Eastern settings so popular at the time, drew an enthusiastic audience, especially among women and young people. His heroes were almost always dark, brooding, solitary young men, hiding deep, painful, personal secrets, who went on adventures to try to escape their own melancholy. It wasn't long before any person or character who fit that description was being referred to as Byronic.

The writer of such dramatic stuff would surely be interested in theater, and Byron found himself on the committee that managed London's Drury Lane Theatre, primarily reading plays being considered for performance. Among the five hundred or so manuscripts Byron flipped through was one by a familiar name: Samuel Taylor Coleridge. Byron had appreciated Coleridge's peculiar genius, especially when it came to poetry with more than a hint of the supernatural. Byron learned that the aging, troubled poet was having difficulties with money—among other things—and he wanted to help. The men set up a meeting. Byron was shocked at how "shabby" his fellow poet looked, but he couldn't deny the power of his work as Coleridge recited line after line of unpublished material. Byron contacted a publisher, showed him Coleridge's "Christabel" and "Kubla Khan," and convinced him to print them and find them a paying audience, even if they weren't quite finished pieces. He produced at least one of Coleridge's forgettable plays. Coleridge in turn provided him with information about werewolves.

One of the perks of Byron's work with the Drury Lane Theatre was getting to meet the actors and actresses, who had a reputation—sometimes well-earned—for being promiscuous. Among them was seventeen-year-old Claire Clairmont. Like Caroline Lamb, Claire became obsessed with the handsome author of so many popular poems. In fact, there was someone she wanted him to meet: Shelley, *almost* a relative of hers by more-or-less marriage, also a poet. She tempted Byron with the poetry—a copy of "Queen Mab"—before she introduced him to Shelley. And it didn't hurt her pursuit that her stepfather was the philosopher William Godwin, someone Byron admired. But first *she* had to meet Byron, and it would be through a letter.

> *If a woman, whose reputation has yet remained unstained, if without guardian or husband to control she should throw herself upon your mercy, with a beating heart she should confess the love she has borne you many years . . . could you betray her or would you be as silent as the grave?*

Claire would need to act quickly, though, if she wanted to get to Lord Byron. He was in the middle of preparations to leave England; selling off some of his possessions, purchasing a huge traveling coach that was a copy of one once owned by Napoleon (it cost five hundred pounds—far more than he could afford), and filling it with luxuries to replace the ones he'd sold. He had barely reached the English coast before his creditors entered Newstead and repossessed everything in it, right down to Byron's tame squirrel.

As he left his homeland forever, Byron said, "I felt that, if what was whispered and muttered and murmured was true—I was unfit for England,—if false—England was unfit for me."

But before Byron fled, Claire got what she wanted from him. When she finally caught up with him again, the final piece of his love-life pentagram would fall into place.

The Poems

WHEN WE TWO PARTED

When we two parted
   In silence and tears,
Half broken-hearted
   To sever for years,
Pale grew thy cheek and cold,
   Colder thy kiss;
Truly that hour foretold
   Sorrow to this.

The dew of the morning
   Sunk chill on my brow—
It felt like the warning
   Of what I feel now.
Thy vows are all broken,
   And light is thy fame;
I hear thy name spoken,
   And share in its shame.

They name thee before me,
   A knell to mine ear;

A shudder comes o'er me—
    Why wert thou so dear?
They know not I knew thee,
    Who knew thee too well—
Long, long shall I rue thee,
    Too deeply to tell.

In secret we met—
    In silence I grieve,
That thy heart could forget,
    Thy spirit deceive.
If I should meet thee
    After long years,
How should I greet thee?—
    With silence and tears.

SHE WALKS IN BEAUTY

1

She walks in beauty, like the night
   Of cloudless climes and starry skies;
And all that's best of dark and bright
   Meet in her aspect and her eyes:
Thus mellowed to that tender light
   Which heaven to gaudy day denies.

2

One shade the more, one ray the less,
   Had half impaired the nameless grace
Which waves in every raven tress,
   Or softly lightens o'er her face;
Where thoughts serenely sweet express
   How pure, how dear their dwelling place.

3

And on that cheek, and o'er that brow,
   So soft, so calm, yet eloquent,
The smiles that win, the tints that glow,
   But tell of days in goodness spent,
A mind at peace with all below,
   A heart whose love is innocent!

Percy Bysshe Shelley

BYRON AND SHELLEY AND THE GIRLS
"You Have Created a Monster"

*A*ll his life Shelley's behavior had been, to put it mildly, a bit twisted. He was the man nineteenth-century essayist William Hazlitt described as having "a fire in his eye, a fever in his blood, a maggot in his brain, a hectic fluttering in his speech." Back in England and trying to cope with a wife who wasn't quite sure what was going on with their marriage, a teenage lover he had to sneak around to see (enough, apparently, to get her pregnant again), and people hounding him for the large amounts of money he owed them, his disturbed—and disturbing—actions escalated. Once again, little paper boats engulfed in flames haunted London's waterways. His sisters Elizabeth and Hellen were still in boarding school; their big brother hatched a plot to kidnap them. He sometimes frightened the wits out of Jane (a.k.a. Claire) Clairmont, choosing bedtime to tell her the lurid horror stories he was so good at making up and staring at her as if he were seeing some ghastly vision beyond. Claire had little sympathy for him. "He says he is unhappy," she wrote in her diary. "God in heaven what has he to be unhappy about!"

Shelley was also a hypochondriac, imagining that his sleep-walking and nightmares, hallucinations and attacks of nerves, were symptoms of everything from the common cold to elephantiasis. His latest medical fear—this time perhaps more real, considering how common it was at the time—was tuberculosis. Byron was actually tactless enough to announce that he wouldn't mind dying of consumption because its victims, as they wasted away, looked so frail and thin and needy. "All the ladies would say 'Look at that poor Byron,'" he mused, "'how interesting he looks in dying.'" The warm winters of Italy, where Byron was living—though not because of consumption—beckoned to Shelley.

Once Shelley turned twenty-one he came into that inheritance he'd been so ready to turn down a few years earlier: one thousand pounds a year for life. Shelley would never really know what it meant to *need* a job, to *need* to sell his poems just to make a living. He made certain some of his grandfather's money would go to Harriet and the children. But he and Mary—and Claire—had plans that didn't include them.

As 1816 began, Mary had a baby she and her lover named William, nicknamed Willmouse. A few months later, they were on their way to Geneva, Switzerland, in pursuit of Lord Byron.

Claire had gotten something very different from a role on stage after her "audition" at the Drury Lane Theatre. She was pregnant.

They left England at the beginning of May, the height of springtime. But in Europe, as they ascended the Alps toward Switzerland, the weather became less and less springlike. Deep snow made some of the mountain roads nearly impassable. At one point, they had to hire ten men to shovel the snow out from in front of their carriage.

The Shelley party was already in Geneva when Byron arrived at his hotel—his ornate carriage probably having struggled through the snowbound Alps, too—so exhausted he put his age as "100" in the register. (The more literal-minded clerk woke him from a deep sleep a half hour later to check whether there had been some mistake.) Playing tricks in the hotel registers seems to have been a game for people like Byron and Shelley. Some guest lists show Shelley's name followed by "democrat, great lover of mankind and atheist." In others, Shelley would sign "Atheist" as his occupation and "L'Enfer" (Hell) as his final destination. That was too much even for Byron. In the years to come, when he came across one of his friend's more audacious entries in his travels, he crossed it out.

Byron had run away from England because he was an object of negative attention. But the Alps couldn't free him from the early version of paparazzi. People who found out where he was staying would aim telescopes at his room, hoping to catch a glimpse of the unsavory activities for which he was famous. He finally rented a much more private house called Villa Diodati, on

Lord Byron

a hill overlooking lovely Lake Leman. And just an eight-minute walk down the hill, right on the lakeshore, was Shelley, along with his entourage.

Those weeks in Geneva were a bonding experience, like summer camp, for the group. They were all living more or less together, spending lots of time in one another's company with nothing pressing to occupy them except leisure. The friendships that were forged on Lake Leman were so strong only death could break them.

The weather turned stormy for a few days that June, keeping everyone indoors, bored. Byron and Shelley could be dangerous—and creative—when they were bored. Between June 16 and 17, as they and their companions sat around talking, they came up with what sounded like a fun parlor game, if you were a writer. They challenged everyone in the group to bring a horror story to their next meeting. (It really was just like summer camp, right down to the ghost stories.) Then they'd read them all aloud and vote for their favorite.

And so, by flickering firelight, as a wild wind whipped sheets of rain against the windows of Villa Diodati, the group assembled to scare each other out of their wits. Byron didn't take the time to write something original. He recited Coleridge's supernatural poem, "Christabel," which sent Shelley into such hallucinations he saw phantom eyes opening in Mary's breasts. He ran screaming out of the room.

One member of Byron's group was John Polidori, technically on the trip as Byron's personal physician. He was insufferably stuffy and not very bright, but he was under the illusion that he was a talented writer, especially after a publisher had offered him five hundred pounds for anticipated memoirs of the trip with the infamous Lord Byron. Behind his back (and perhaps even to his face), Byron called Polidori Dr. PollyDolly. Polidori outdid himself with a story he called "The Vampyr."

But the surprise of the evening was from "the Maie," nineteen-year-old Mary Godwin. Not for nothing had she been hanging around with a man obsessed with the evil side of new scientific discoveries. She took the very real studies of electricity, including its apparent power to bring dead things back to life, and tweaked them into one of the greatest horror stories of all time, *Frankenstein*. Her upbringing in a house full of literary people showed, too. She peppered her story with quotes from works by Coleridge and Byron. Byron returned the favor by praising what became the ultimate gothic novel: "Methinks it is a wonderful work for a girl of nineteen,—*not* nineteen, indeed, at that time." Even Shelley was impressed enough to offer to help his girlfriend edit the story and prepare it for publication.

Mary Godwin Shelley

On Lake Leman, Shelley and Byron found they had more in common than writing. They both enjoyed sailing on the crystal waters right at their doorstep, when the stormy weather let up long enough for them to take a boat out. Just a week after the night of ghost stories, they sailed out into a clear, bright afternoon—which didn't last. A storm was coming up, and fast, too fast for them to get back to shore. As the wind buffeted their little sailboat and the waves crashing onto the deck threatened to overturn it, Byron made a discovery as scary as any of those horror stories they'd been making up. If the boat went down, Shelley would go right down with it. He'd never learned to swim. Byron was an accomplished swimmer. If he ended up in the lake, he'd probably be able to swim safely to the shore. He came up with ideas for what his friend should do if their boat capsized: grab an oar and float, or let Byron himself, a strong enough swimmer for two, hold on to him and pull him to safety. Shelley calmly declined. Never mind the oar. Never mind trying to save him. The wild waves could do with him as they would. It was up to the sea whether he would live or die.

However, that night, safely ashore, Shelley wrote his will.

Spending a summer by the shores of Lake Leman with Lord Byron was lots of fun, but that wasn't why Shelley and his group were in Switzerland. Claire wanted Byron to accept responsibility for the baby she was carrying. She hoped he'd invite her to live with him. It wasn't happening. Byron wasn't so sure Claire's baby was his. He'd consider doing something for it once it was born, maybe. He was so serious in his reluctance, even Shelley—who wasn't exactly the model of paternal responsibility—assured Claire he'd take care of her while she was pregnant and would do what he could to provide for the baby. But in the meantime, they'd return to England.

A few weeks later, Fanny Godwin—quiet, complacent, domestic Fanny, her father's favorite—checked into a hotel room and killed herself with an overdose of opium. She went to her grave alone. Not a single one of the Godwins could bring themselves to attend the funeral. Of course they were grieving, but they were also dealing with the fact that a philosopher, a man who seemed to know all the answers and was eager to give them to so many others, had apparently failed his own stepdaughter in some way. Friends and relatives, even Fanny's stepbrother, Charles, were told that she'd taken a trip to Ireland, had taken ill there, and suddenly died. Not until six months later did the truth about her death begin to come out.

Then, while Fanny Godwin's suicide was still fresh in everyone's minds, Harriet Shelley disappeared. Her husband learned her fate in a letter from a friend. Five weeks after she went missing, her body was discovered floating in the shallow waters of the Serpentine, where her husband had once sailed paper boats. She had obviously been in the water for several days. Suicide was suspected. And, the letter confided, Harriet had been pregnant at the time of her death.

Harriet had left a note saying that her two children, Charles and Ianthe, were to stay with her sister, Eliza, until more permanent arrangements could be made. Shelley consulted a lawyer, who told him that he might be more likely to get custody of them if he were married. Harriet's body was barely cold in the grave when Percy Bysshe Shelley and Mary Godwin, his lover, the mother of his *other* children, became husband and wife. But Harriet's parents, the Westbrooks, refused to see their grandchildren released to the man whose insensitivity had driven Harriet to her death. The courts sent Charles and Ianthe to be raised by a clergyman named Dr. Thomas Hume. The Westbrooks and Shelley would be allowed to visit them. There is no record Shelley ever did so.

Just a few days after her stepsister's wedding, Claire had her baby. Immediately, friends whisked the child away. When they reappeared to visit Claire and the Shelleys, it was with a new "cousin" Claire had selflessly volunteered to raise, a little girl she named Alba. Back in Switzerland, Byron's nickname had been Albe, more or less the local pronunciation of his initials, L. B.

Shelley wrote his friend, letting him know that he had another daughter. Byron wanted nothing more to do with Claire, but he did agree to provide for the girl's support and education. He was living now in Venice, in a grand house called the Palazzo Mocenigo, right on the Grand Canal. He shared the space with fourteen servants; a menagerie that included horses, monkeys, peacocks, and an assortment of dogs; and a string of mistresses. When the time came, there would surely be enough room for a toddler.

Shelley and his new wife found that London agreed with them. He was whipping out long (but not very successful) poems that mixed themes of government, religion, and love. She was basking in positive reviews for *Frankenstein*. Mozart's opera *Don Giovanni* was the hit of the city's cultural season, and Shelley sat through it night after night. Byron was working on a series of poems about the same scandalous character featured in the opera, the promiscuous adventurer Don Juan, so it was a natural favorite for Shelley.

Shelley was also forging friendships with another set of writers and poets. The most talented among them was a young man named John Keats.

The Poems

TO NIGHT

by Percy Bysshe Shelley

Swiftly walk o'er the western wave,
    Spirit of Night!
Out of the misty eastern cave
Where, all the long and lone daylight
Thou wovest dreams of joy and fear,
Which make thee terrible and dear,
    Swift be thy flight!

Wrap thy form in a mantle grey,
    Star-inwrought!
Blind with thine hair the eyes of day,
Kiss her until she be wearied out—
Then wander o'er City and sea and land,
Touching all with thine opiate wand—
    Come, long-sought!

When I arose and saw the dawn
    I sighed for thee;
When Light rode high, and the dew was gone,

And noon lay heavy on flower and tree,
And the weary Day turned to his rest,
Lingering like an unloved guest,
    I sighed for thee.

Thy brother Death came, and cried,
    Wouldst thou me?
Thy sweet child Sleep, the filmy-eyed,
Murmured like a noontide bee,
Shall I nestle near thy side?
Wouldst thou me? and I replied,
    No, not thee!

Death will come when thou art dead,
    Soon, too soon—
Sleep will come when thou art fled;
Of neither would I ask the boon
I ask of thee, beloved Night—
Swift be thine approaching flight,
    Come soon, soon!

John Keats

KEATS

"Tadpole of the Lakes"

*L*ike so many of his fellow poets, the key event in the early life of John Keats was the death of a parent—his father, Thomas Keats. Thomas had met his wife, Frances Jennings, while working at her father's stables. After they were married, he continued to take care of horses at a London inn called the Swan and Hoop. They had four children, ranging from nine-year-old John to one-year-old Fanny, when Thomas died in a riding accident.

Mrs. Keats remarried, but her new husband, William Rawlings, was not interested in a ready-made family. All those children had to go. It was a bad match. Rawlings and Mrs. Keats broke up fairly quickly, and she went to join her children, who were living with their grandparents. Unfortunately, by leaving her husband, she gave up all legal claim to anything Thomas Keats had left her in his will. When her father died, he left a comfortable inheritance to his grandchildren, but the man who was watching the finances for the Keats children was Richard Abbey, a tea merchant with, apparently, no imagination and no great understanding of youngsters. He insisted that the wording of old Mr. Jennings's will was unclear. The Keats children might each get their money as they turned twenty-one or they might have to wait until they had *all* turned twenty-one. Abbey chose the latter interpretation of the will. Meanwhile, the Keatses were raised as if they were very poor.

John was athletic, shy, temperamental, and obviously bright. In school, he carried off all sorts of prizes for his writing. He was also very sensitive. When he was fifteen, while at school, he was told that his mother had died of consumption. He hid himself in the small cubby under his teacher's desk. He fit there comfortably: He was only five feet tall.

The headmaster at John's school admired good writing and freedom of thought and expression. He subscribed to a liberal magazine called *The Examiner,* published by Leigh Hunt, a classmate of Coleridge's. Through that publication, students like Keats became acquainted with the latest trends in poetry. Hunt was not a great poet himself. The only piece of his that readers today might be vaguely familiar with is a poem called "Jenny Kissed Me." But he made it a point to befriend and socialize with the up-and-coming writers of the day. Byron would monopolize the Hunt children's rocking horse when he visited. Shelley gave Hunt money—a bad habit, since he lived so extravagantly he really didn't have enough money to lend.

Before coming to England, the Hunt family had lived in Barbados and Philadelphia, but still loyal to King George, they had decided not to remain in those revolting former colonies. Yet the freethinking colonial spirit had rubbed off on the Hunts. When Leigh and his brother John started their magazine, they were not afraid to print what they believed to be true, no matter how much trouble it might get them into.

They wrote that the Prince Regent, King George III's underage son who would eventually rule England, was a libertine—a man with loose morals and expensive tastes and the money and power to indulge any and all of his vices. And it was true. At one of the prince's many parties, the decoration that set high society talking was an indoor artificial stream full of live goldfish. It alone cost one hundred twenty thousand pounds—at a time when ordinary workers in England were having trouble making ends meet. Nevertheless, the Hunt brothers were accused of libel and threatened with two years in prison and a fine of five hundred pounds, a hefty sum. Leigh Hunt chose to go to jail rather than take back his accusation. It wasn't a bad choice: He picked out a lovely rose-trellis wallpaper for his cell, painted the ceiling to look like the sky, installed blinds on the windows, brought in his piano, had access to any books he wanted, invited his family in and out as if they were guests in an apartment, and even grew a small garden outside. It was a pretty cushy prison sentence.

This was the man whose magazine probably introduced John

Keats to the major poets and poetry of his era. For Keats was born just three years before Wordsworth and Coleridge published the first edition of *Lyrical Ballads*. To young Keats, Lord Byron and Sir Walter Scott were the literary kings of the day. Byron was at the height of his infamy while Keats was in school; one of his first poems was a reaction to reading part of "Childe Harold." And as Keats was choosing a trade, Byron and Shelley and their entourage were spending their enchanted summer on the shores of Lake Leman.

Keats started writing poetry around 1814, but even he knew it wasn't very good. It was mostly bad imitations of other poets' work. His idol was Thomas Chatterton, who had died about forty years earlier. People in the mid-1700s were fascinated by anything ancient or medieval, even if it was *fake* ancient or medieval. When he was still a teenager, Chatterton had published poems he claimed to have discovered, poems by a medieval monk named Thomas Rowley. The spelling, the choice of words, the rhymes and meters, all seemed authentic—at first glance. But further research proved that there was no such person as Thomas Rowley. Or, more precisely, Thomas Rowley *was* Thomas Chatterton, who had read so much old poetry he'd become (almost) an expert at imitating its style. Once his secret was revealed, he lost interest in life. Chatterton committed suicide at the age of seventeen by taking a fatal dose of arsenic. A brilliant mind, a blazing talent, a life tragically cut short: he was a natural role model for young Romantic wannabes.

Of all the people Keats knew, Richard Abbey was most displeased with his ward's desire to be a poet. Abbey wanted the Keats boys to take up a trade, as he had. They didn't have to be tea merchants, but they should be able to get a steady job that would support them and, eventually, a family. He'd taken Keats out of school when he turned fifteen—right around the time of his mother's death—and apprenticed him to a surgeon-apothecary, where he learned to mix and dispense medicines, set bones, and pull teeth. (He also had to take an apprentice's oath that, for five years, he would not get married or gamble, and would not set foot in a tavern or a theater.)

After a period of training, Keats began attending classes at St. Guy's Hospital in London, where he would sometimes stand in an audience of students, watching an operation being performed on a patient who had not been given any sort of anaesthetic. Laughing gas was just coming into vogue, but as more of a novelty than a medical aid, as Robert Southey knew well. Keats spent most of his time during lectures doodling flowers into the margins of his notebooks. His training would not allow him to be a physician, actually diagnosing and caring for patients. That would mean years of study, and Abbey was not about to part with the money it would cost. But it would prepare Keats to take the licensing exam to become a surgeon-apothecary. Meanwhile, he worked in the hospital as a dresser, a sort of nurse whose responsibility was removing bandages, cleaning the pus-filled and sometimes gangrenous wounds beneath, and putting on fresh bandages. This had to be done twice a day; there were no such things as antiseptics or antibiotics to keep wounds from becoming infected.

Then, while he was studying and working as a dresser and appearing to do everything just as Abbey wanted him to, Keats had a poem, a sonnet entitled "On Solitude," published in Leigh Hunt's *Examiner*. Abbey had not stifled his ward's dream at all.

Keats passed the exam to become an apothecary in July of 1816. But the law stated that he was not allowed to begin practicing until he was twenty-one, which wouldn't be until October 31. So he did what anyone his age would do between completing school and starting a job: He went to the beach. He tried out the new "bathing machine," which allowed people to enjoy a dip in cool ocean water while protecting their modesty. A large vehicle, something like a delivery truck, would be wheeled into the water until it was two or three hundred yards offshore. Then its door would open, an umbrellalike contraption would come down, and bathers could climb up and down a ladder into the bracing water without exposing themselves to the whole world.

He also toured Scotland. His sister, Fanny, who was then twelve, enjoyed his little verses, so from Scotland he wrote her:

> *There was a naughty boy,*
>   *And a naughty boy was he,*
> *He ran away to Scotland*
>   *The people for to see—*
> *There he found*

That the ground
Was as hard
That a yard
Was as long,
That a song
Was as merry,
That a cherry
Was as red,
That lead
Was as weighty,
That fourscore
Was as eighty,
That a door
Was as wooden
As in England—
So he stood in his shoes
   And he wonder'd,
   He wonder'd
As he stood in his
   Shoes and he wonder'd.

Back in London, Keats dropped in on a friend and found him reading George Chapman's translation of Homer's *Iliad* and *Odyssey*. Keats read a bit of it, and loved it—so much that he was moved to write a sonnet about it the next morning. He wrote from six to nine A.M.; by ten he had sent a copy off to his friend. It remains one of his most famous pieces.

But it was a sonnet, just fourteen lines long. Keats was determined to write something longer, more epic. "Did our great Poets ever write short pieces?" he would say. It was something he would try to accomplish all his life. Once he even set himself a goal of four thousand lines, and worked at it every day. Only one of those four thousand lines from *Endymion* is remotely memorable: "A thing of beauty is a joy forever."

Now that he was a published poet, Keats began to affect a distinctive literary look. He let his auburn hair grow long onto the open collars of his shirts, and he sported a scarf, loose-fitting jackets, baggy pants. When Keats's birthday came and went and he was still working in the hospital as a dresser and rooming with his brothers, Richard Abbey asked him why he had not yet acted like an adult and set himself up as an apothecary. Keats replied that he had decided to become a poet instead. He was even entering his poetry in contests, hoping to make some money. (But he wasn't winning.) Abbey suggested one alternative after another: a tea merchant, like himself, though not with the same company; a hatmaker; perhaps, for a young man who loved literature so much, a bookseller. He didn't think much of poets, but admitted that even Lord Byron "does say true things now and then"—such as when he wrote that literature was no way to make a living.

Leigh Hunt, however, had written an article listing John Keats as one of the three bright lights of a "new school of poetry" (the other two being Shelley and the now-forgotten J. H. Reynolds). It was high praise from a magazine that had referred to Coleridge's poem "Christabel" as "evidence of insanity." That praise was enough to give Keats the encouragement he needed.

Leigh Hunt nicknamed his latest discovery Junkets (as in *John Keats* said very quickly) and began introducing him to the other creative types whose friendship he cultivated. Hunt, his wife, and their numerous children lived in Hampstead Heath, on the outskirts of London. One of the men Keats met at Hunt's Hampstead soirees was the painter Benjamin Robert Haydon. Haydon was a big, blustering, somewhat disheveled man who created big, pompous, busy paintings. He liked to drop images of his friends and acquaintances into his works. If you look closely at Haydon's gigantic painting *Christ's Entry into Jerusalem* (it measures thirteen by fifteen feet; the frame alone weighs six hundred pounds), you can catch a glimpse in the crowd of William Wordsworth, as well as John Keats.

Keats mentioned to his new friend that he admired Wordsworth's work, particularly "Lines Composed a Few Miles Above Tintern Abbey." Haydon sent Wordsworth a copy of one of Keats's poems and finally set up a meeting between the two poets. Keats read aloud a bit of his four-thousand-liner, *Endymion,* an excerpt about the Greek god Pan. Wordsworth declared it "a pretty piece of Paganism," which Keats took (probably correctly) as meaning that the older man—forty-seven at the time—wasn't impressed with the work of this young pup. When he published his first book of poetry, Keats sent Wordsworth a copy inscribed "To W. Wordsworth with the Author's sincere Reverence." Years later it was found on Wordsworth's bookshelf. Books in the early 1800s were bound in such a way that the first person to read them had to slit the pages apart. Most of Wordsworth's copy of Keats was conspicuously unslit.

It took one holiday season to tarnish the hero worship Keats felt for Wordsworth, although he would continue to admire the man's work. The two poets, one young, one old, found themselves attending the same round of holiday parties. In fact, sometimes Coleridge was also among the guests, although never when Keats was present. Asra—Sarah Hutchinson, the great love of Coleridge's life, whom he hadn't seen for seven years—found herself on some of those guest lists, too. It was uncomfortable when all those people with so much unresolved and painful history suddenly saw each other after a very long time. But Wordsworth didn't make it easier. At one end of the long table set for the holidays, the partygoers would hear Coleridge's nasal, mesmerizing preacher's voice with its strong Devon accent reciting Wordsworth's poetry from memory. And at the other end they'd hear Wordsworth, his Cumbrian accent as distinctive as Coleridge's, also reciting poetry from memory.

His own.

Keats found the Wordsworth he met at those holiday parties too full of himself. He had to be the center of attention—and if he wasn't, he'd find a way to draw all eyes and ears to himself. No one else stood a chance when Wordsworth was working the room. Certainly not a short, sickly boy with a handful of mediocre verses to show for himself. And definitely not a disheveled, over-the-hill drug addict.

Robert Haydon also took Keats to the British Museum to see the Elgin marbles, which were the talk of London. Britain's Lord Elgin had brought back a pretty big souvenir from his trip to Greece: huge marble friezes from the Parthenon in Athens. Lord Byron had criticized what amounted to theft of a national treasure, but none of that mattered to Lord Elgin, who pocketed twenty-five thousand pounds from the English government in appreciation for his stolen souvenirs. Keats returned so often to the museum to study the depictions of gods and goddesses, a friend noticed and assured him his appreciation for their beauty was well-placed: "Yes, I believe, Mr. Keats, we may admire these works safely."

Lord Elgin was not the only person with a healthy disrespect for the historical. Byron had carved his initials into the marble columns of an ancient temple outside Athens. And Keats, paying a visit to that most hallowed shrine for English writers, Shakespeare's birthplace of Stratford-upon-Avon, scribbled his name onto a wall.

The Elgin marbles were not the only pieces of stolen antiquity arriving in England at the time. Wonders were also pouring in from Egypt: the Rosetta stone, a statue of the Egyptian pharaoh Ramses II. One evening at Leigh Hunt's home, the poets in attendance were given a challenge to write a poem about the source of all these curiosities. The winner would be honored with a crown of laurel leaves. Keats was there, and so was Percy Shelley. Keats didn't produce on the spur of the moment. Shelley's attempt was a bit better. But a short time later, out of that Egyptian inspiration came Shelley's "Ozymandias," which of course was snatched up for publication in the *Examiner.*

About Shelley and Keats, Hunt would recall, "Keats did not take to Shelley as kindly as Shelley did to him . . . [and] Keats being a little too sensitive on the score of his origin, felt inclined to see in every man of birth a sort of natural enemy." Some literary magazines (though not Hunt's) put down what they called the "Cockney school" of poetry and complained that the lower classes were trying to get in on the act. Now just about *anyone*— even a *dresser,* heaven forbid!—could say he was a poet. What Keats was saying was, "O for a Life of Sensations Rather than Thoughts!" What the critics said was that his poetry was sensual to the point of indecency—even Lord Byron called it "mental masturbation." But Shelley saw potential in his young friend. He read the early poems and advised Keats not to be in too much of a hurry to publish them, to wait until he had more, and better, work to share. Keats ignored the advice. But Shelley was right. People were actually returning copies of Keats's first book to the shop that stocked it. This was the book that Wordsworth barely opened. Only the other Keats boys thought everything their big brother did was wonderful; they didn't understand what he was writing about, but he was their hero.

Shelley was also right that Keats's work would improve as he matured. He not only wrote poetry, he thought deeply about the *process* of writing poetry and what it meant to live as a poet, what it meant to be self-aware, all very philosophical concepts.

I go among the feilds [sic] and catch a glimpse of a stoat or a fieldmouse peeping out of the withered grass—the creature hath a purpose and its eyes are bright with it—I go amongst the buildings of a city and I see a Man hurrying along—to what? The Creature has a purpose and his eyes are bright with it. But then as Wordsworth says, "we have all one human heart."

The young poet was developing a theory he called "Negative Capability." A poet, he felt, should be able to hold two contradictory ideas in his mind at the same time, not judging one over the other, just accepting them both. It was a concept that explained how a writer could get into the head of a character who was completely different from him- or herself, who could do things the author would never dream of—and write about that person, his actions, his choices, his feelings, with conviction and understanding.

Keats had his own idiosyncrasies when it came to writing. He dashed his poems off quickly, but not the way Byron did, just pouring out feelings with little or no revision. Keats didn't wait until he was finished to edit and fine-tune his work; he did it as he went along, which was what made the writing seem to go quickly. The literary devices that make Keats's poems so musical and distinctive didn't just happen. Keats thought about things like alliteration and assonance and turned the music captive in his words to their advantage. When he had writer's block, he would pretend he was getting ready for a night on the town—he washed up, dressed in his best. It worked. He never left the room, but he felt as if he had, and he was able to get back into his writing with new enthusiasm. Other times, he would work on a completely different poem. Success with one often led to success with the other. He wondered sometimes whether other writers used some of his tricks—for instance, in what position was Shakespeare sitting when he wrote the immortal line, "To be, or not to be"?

Keats's connections introduced him to a musical circle of friends, too. He was often invited to dinner by Vincent Novello. Novello himself wasn't known as a musician, but as a music publisher. The composers whose works he'd published included Joseph Haydn and Wolfgang Mozart. Sometimes Keats and company would play at being an orchestra. But they wouldn't use real instruments; they'd imitate the sounds those instruments made, a little like what modern vocalist Bobby McFerrin does when he bops along with a classical piece. Keats's "instrument" was Mozart's favorite: the low-pitched, farting bassoon.

Then harsh reality struck. John's brother Tom had fallen ill and was getting sicker and sicker with what was clearly consumption. Another brother, George, had been caring for him, but George and his wife wanted to immigrate to America. (They eventually opened a flour and lumber mill in Kentucky and almost went into the riverboat business with bird-painter-to-be John James Audubon.) John was off on a walking tour of Scotland and the Lakes in northern England—642 miles altogether.

In the Lakes, he tried to visit Wordsworth, but the poet was out campaigning for a local political candidate. His experience in Scotland wasn't much more satisfying. Keats wrote, "I have got wet through day after day, eaten oat cake, & drank whiskey, walked up to my knees in Bog, got a sore throat. . . . We have been taken for Spectacle venders, Razor sellers, Jewellers, traveling linen drapers, Spies, Excisemen, & many things else." When he got back to London from this cheery vacation, Tom became his responsibility.

In a stuffy, airless flat, the windows shut tight so not a breath of chill breeze would touch Tom, John Keats nursed his brother through the last weeks of his brief life. Richard Abbey was still trying to rule the Keats children's lives. Until it was obvious that Tom was dying, he refused to allow Fanny to say a last good-bye to her brother until it was almost too late. John would be there, and according to Abbey, a respectable young lady should not be seen in the company of a poet. Tom Keats was nineteen years old when he died with John by his side. Keats then walked in a daze from their flat to the Hampstead home of his friend, Charles Brown, who took over the sad task of letting friends and family know of the death.

It was through Charles Brown that John Keats met the love of his life. Brown's home in Hampstead, Wentworth House, was a duplex. Among the people he rented one side of the house to was a widow, Mrs. Brawne, with three children. The late Mr. Brawne had been a cousin of Beau Brummel, a London socialite who set the standard of fashion for the well-dressed young, urban gentleman in the era of the scandalous Prince Regent. Mr. Brawne had died of consumption. The oldest of the Brawne children was Fanny, a teenager who lived up to the Brummel reputation. She was a petite and pretty blue-eyed brunette. But there was a brain in that pretty little head and a witty tongue in that sweet mouth. Fanny Brawne was planning to get away from England, to live her life on the Continent, so she learned to speak French and German fluently. Fashion was in her blood, but she didn't just dress the part; she kept folders full of illustrations as complete as any reference book on clothing trends through history. Her taste in literature ran more to sensational gothic novels and Byron's scandalous story-poems than to the sort of sensitive, soul-searching sonnets Keats was writing. But when they met, this girl full of life and energy and irreverence fascinated him.

In a letter to George, now in America, Keats described Fanny. "[She] is I think beautiful and elegant, graceful, silly, fashionable and strange—we have a little tiff now and then—and she behaves a little better, or I must have sheered off. . . . [S]he is ignorant—monstrous in her behavior flying out in all directions, calling people such names—that I was forced lately to make use of the term <u>Minx</u>—this I think no[t] from any innate vice but from a penchant she has for acting stylishly." The two began exchanging love letters in 1819. He was twenty-three. She was nineteen. That fall, John secretly gave Fanny an engagement ring.

Love had opened Keats's literary floodgates. Within just a few months in 1819, he wrote his most memorable poems, one after the other, rewording and reworking lines as he wrote so the work went quickly. Out poured "Bright Star" (which may or may not have been about Fanny Brawne), "Eve of Saint Agnes," "La Belle Dame sans Merci," "Ode on a Grecian Urn," "Ode to Melancholy." "Ode to a Nightingale" was completed, perfect, in a single morning. One day in September, Keats went for a walk and wrote to a friend, "How beautiful the season is now—How fine the air. A temperate sharpness about it . . . I never lik'd stubble fields so much as now—Aye better than the chilly green of the spring. Somehow a stubble plain looks warm—in the same way that some pictures look warm—this struck me so much in my sunday's walk that I composed upon it." The poem he "composed upon it" was "To Autumn," so intense in its descriptions you can smell overripe fruit and crisp fall leaves when you read it. Using an image involving one sense to stimulate another sense— like catching a pleasant scent when you imagine a visual picture— is a literary device called synesthesia. Keats was becoming a master of it.

Life looked good for John Keats. Poetry was pouring out of him. He had a loving fiancée—a little hard to handle, perhaps, but bright and pretty. But one day, out on Hampstead Heath, he came across a man who was no stranger to poetry, or to the difficulties life can throw at you. Samuel Taylor Coleridge was living in Highgate, a neighborhood not too far from Hampstead. He had aged, and addiction had taken a lot out of him, but he was still a walker, and the grassy, wild hills of the Heath were a perfect place to walk. The two tramped along together for a while, talking—typically for Coleridge—about a weird combination of philosophy and nightmares. When they parted, Keats shook Coleridge's hand. Coleridge shuddered. After Keats's drama had played out, Coleridge recalled thinking, "There is death in that hand."

The miracle year of 1819 rolled into the winter of 1820. On one of those deceptively balmy January thaw days, Keats went out to do some errands. He left his heavy coat at home and made himself comfortable on one of the outside seats of the coach to save a bit of money. The weather changed suddenly; the freezing winter air chilled him to the bone. He barely staggered home, already flushed and delirious with fever, and collapsed onto his bed, coughing convulsively. And suddenly, on his pillow he saw a spot of wet, deep red. He'd cared for Tom. He'd worked in a hospital and had enough medical training to know what he was looking at. "I know the colour of that blood;—it is arterial blood;—I cannot be deceived in that colour;—that drop of blood is my death-warrant;—I must die."

He could not bear to put Fanny Brawne through the ordeal he'd been through with Tom. He didn't want her to watch him "making [his] exit like a frog in a frost. I can bear to die—I cannot bear to leave her," Keats wrote. Yet he was living in Charles Brown's Hampstead duplex, with the Brawnes right on the other side of the wall. Every day he and Fanny exchanged little notes. Clueless doctors tried bleeding him—cutting a vein to drain some blood, which they thought was a universal cure. They advised him to become a vegetarian or perhaps not to eat at all. They recommended drinking seawater, wearing flannel. They prescribed total rest, not even writing. Some insisted Keats's problem wasn't tuberculosis at all but a stomach ailment, or maybe just a case of nerves.

No one—at least in England—had the foggiest idea that tuberculosis was highly contagious, that it spread from one person to another like wildfire via the phlegm and blood the patient was coughing up. Doctors claimed the disease was hereditary, but neither genes nor coincidence were the real reason that relatives of consumptives who were nursed in the recommended warm, windowless, airless rooms almost invariably contracted consumption themselves, and very quickly. John Keats's lungs were probably full of tuberculosis germs from his time with his brother Tom. He lived an active life and didn't take very good care of himself, continuing to tramp about on long walking trips in the rain and cold, even with a sore throat. Something set off the dormant germs and made them active, fatally active. Eventually, George Keats—another of Tom's dedicated nurses—would die of the same disease.

Charles Brown wasn't about to be a nurse. He planned his usual summer vacation and told Keats he'd be renting out their rooms. Sicker and sicker, Keats moved in with the Hunts. Even the Brawnes took him in for a while, hard as that must have been for Fanny. One doctor then gave Keats a ray of hope. Some consumptives improved when they got away from England's chilly rains and mists and traveled to a place with a warmer climate—say, Italy. That's what Shelley had planned when he suspected he was sickening with tuberculosis.

Shelley heard that his friend was ill, probably with consumption, and invited him south. He was in Pisa; Keats should come for a visit. After reading Keats's latest poems, he wrote to Mrs. Hunt, "Where is Keats now? I am anxiously expecting him in Italy where I shall take care to bestow every possible attention on him. I consider his a most valuable life & am deeply interested in his safety. I intend to be the physician both to his body & his soul, to keep the one warm & to teach the other Greek and Spanish. I am aware indeed in part that I am nourishing a rival who will far surpass me and this is an additional motive & will be an added pleasure." He had no idea just how close to death Keats was.

Keats asked Richard Abbey for some money so he could make the journey that might save his life. Abbey refused. Desperate, Keats sold the copyright to his poems and booked passage on a ship called the *Maria Crowther*. With him, bound for Rome, came Joseph Severn, an aspiring painter Keats had met a few years earlier. They didn't know each other all that well but had a few things in common, like an appreciation for walks on Hampstead Heath. Severn thought some time in Rome might give him a chance to study the great classical art in that city. How hard could it be to act as traveling companion for a young man, even a frail-looking young man?

Storms lashed at the ship all through the journey to Italy, but that was hardly the worst of the hardships Keats and Severn had to face. They shared a damp, cramped cabin with not just the captain of the *Maria Crowther* and her first mate, but also with a Miss Cotterell and her companion, Mrs. Pidgeon. Like Keats, Miss Cotterell was suffering from consumption and was on her way to Italy in search of a healthier climate, but her symptoms were different from Keats's. He always felt cold and wanted the window closed. The heat and stuffiness made her faint, so she would open the window for fresh air. As soon as she did, Keats would begin to cough up blood.

To amuse himself during the voyage, Keats read the latest installment of Lord Byron's comic serial poem *Don Juan*. It contained a scene of a shipwreck—after which the survivors turned to cannibalism. Keats was aghast. "This gives me the most horrid idea of human nature, that a man like Byron should have exhausted all the pleasures of the world so completely that there was nothing left for him but to laugh and gloat over the most solemn and heart-rending scenes of human misery."

Things didn't improve when the *Maria Crowther* finally reached shore in Naples. Back in London, there had been an outbreak of typhus, and all English ships coming into the harbor were put into quarantine for ten days. So, for another week and a half, Keats and Miss Cotterell argued over their cabin's window. The passengers were finally allowed to go ashore on October 31, 1820: Keats's twenty-fifth birthday. He and Severn quickly set

out for Rome. They took a second-floor apartment in a neighborhood frequented by English travelers, looking out over the
famed Spanish steps.

Italy was seeing a lot of these consumptives from up north,
and locals were beginning to appreciate the seriousness of the
disease and how contagious its victims were. Severn did not dare
tell the landlady, Signora Angeletti, just what his friend and
roommate was suffering from. If he did, she would have had everything in their apartment—every stick of furniture, every article
of clothing, every book and pen, canvas and brush—burned.
Unfortunately for Keats but fortunately for the roommates, a
doctor insisted that consumption was not Keats's problem. He
could barely eat the bread and milk Severn brought to his bed
for the pains in his stomach; therefore the trouble, the doctor
said, was with his digestive system, not his lungs. When Signora
Angeletti finally saw through the pretense, Severn assured her
(with fingers crossed behind his back) that Keats was bedridden,
totally confined to his own room. In Severn's living area were his
painting materials, books, piano. Sometimes Keats *did* enjoy sitting in there, though.

And so began Keats's "posthumous existence," as he called
it in a letter to Charles Brown. Severn had a right to call what he
was going through a living death, too. He'd left England expecting to spend time strolling among Rome's ruins or studying great
works of art in her museums, then coming home to paint and
provide some companionship for Keats. Instead, he found himself as live-in nurse for a dying man. Severn sat up with him night

and day; Keats was in too much pain to sleep. He also insisted that a candle burn through the night, which meant that Severn would have to get up every few hours to light a fresh one. The artist set up a contraption—what Keats called a "fairy lamp-lighter"—where one candle would light the next before it burned out, so the exhausted painter could get some sleep himself. (It's not surprising Keats wanted a light in the room. His fireplace was decorated with leering, gargoyle-like faces that would have given even a healthy person nightmares.) Always in need of money, Severn cooked or negotiated with the landlady for meals. It's pretty hard to ruin basic Italian food, but she managed. Severn had to throw a dish of her inedible slop out the window before she would give her boarders something a little better.

Letters arrived from Fanny Brawne. Keats could not bear to open and read them. They would only cause him more pain than he was already suffering. They were placed in a little box for safekeeping. But this didn't stop a frazzled Joseph Severn from writing one day to Fanny:

> *For Three weeks I have never left him—I have sat up at night—I have read to him nearly all day & even in the night—I light the fire, make his breakfast & sometimes am obliged to cook—make his bed and even sweep the room. I can have these things done, but never at the time when they ought & must be done—so that you will see my alternative—what enrages me most is making a fire I blow—blow—for an hour—the smoke comes fuming*

*out—my kettle falls over on the burning sticks—no
stove—Keats calling me to be with him—the fire catching my hands & the door bell ringing—all these to one
quite unused and not at all capable—with the want of
every proper material. . . .*

It's an experience—and a feeling—home caregivers even
today can easily understand.

Keats tried to explain to Severn what would happen to him
physically as he neared the end. But there is a big difference
between understanding that kind of suffering intellectually and
watching it firsthand. Keats's mouth was always full of blood, so
dark it was almost black. He drooled it, coughed it, spit it, vom-
ited it. Severn worried that his friend might commit suicide just
to put an end to his pain, so he hid all the knives—and the laudanum he had on hand. When Keats begged for the drug, Severn
refused. Severn admitted he'd never seen a person die before.
That may not seem unusual today, but it was in the early 1800s,
when sick or elderly people were more likely to die at home, surrounded by family, than in a hospital. Nursing homes and hos-
pices didn't even exist. Keats said all Severn could do was be
there and be strong for him; he'd try to make his exit a quick and
easy one.

Severn was there with his friend John Keats late on the night
of Friday, February 23, 1821. The twenty-five-year-old poet died
in his friend's arms, surrounded by the beloved books he'd been

far too sick to read for so long. He was buried three days later in a spot Severn had located in Rome's Protestant Cemetery, a plot where violets—Keats's favorite flower—flourished in the spring. Fanny Brawne's letters, still unopened, still in their box, were buried beside him. Everything that remained in Keats's room, everything he touched or breathed on during the months he was sick, was burned.

All Keats wanted on his tombstone were the words "Here lies one whose name was writ in water." His friend Charles Brown couldn't resist adding a preface: "This Grave contains all that was Mortal, of a YOUNG ENGLISH POET who, on his Death Bed, in the Bitterness of his Heart at the Malicious Power of his Enemies, Desired these Words to be engraven on his Tomb Stone." Keats was barely cold in the ground before a myth began to spring up that he'd been killed by the negative review a magazine had given his work. To give up on life and waste away because one's creativity was unappreciated and misunderstood sounded much more interesting—Romantic!—than dying of a common disease like consumption.

Even Byron played a part in circulating the myth. In one canto, or chapter, of *Don Juan*, he rhymed:

> *John Keats, who was killed off by one critique,*
> *   Just as he really promised something great, . . .*
> *'Tis strange the mind, that very fiery particle,*
> *Should let itself be snuffed out by an article.*

As he learned more of the story behind the poet's last months, however, Byron changed his mind and asked his publisher to please omit any lines that cast John Keats in a bad light.

Shelley's memorial to his talented young friend was more respectful—a poetic elegy entitled "Adonais."

As for Fanny Brawne, John Keats was apparently a hard act to follow. She went into mourning, and friends and family must have believed she would die an old maid. She finally married twelve years after Keats's death.

John Keats was the first of the major Romantic poets to die. But mortality was teaching its harsh lessons to his fellow writers in its own way.

The Poems

On First Looking into Chapman's Homer

Much have I traveled in the realms of gold,
   And many goodly states and kingdoms seen;
   Round many western islands have I been
Which bards in fealty to Apollo hold.
Oft of one wide expanse had I been told
   That deep-browed Homer ruled as his demesne;
   Yet did I never breathe its pure serene
Till I heard Chapman speak out loud and bold:
Then felt I like some watcher of the skies
   When a new planet swims into his ken;
Or like stout Cortez when with eagle eyes
   He stared at the Pacific—and all his men
Looked at each other with a wild surmise—
   Silent, upon a peak in Darien.

WHEN I HAVE FEARS

When I have fears that I may cease to be
   Before my pen has gleaned my teeming brain,
Before high-piléd books, in charact'ry,
   Hold like rich garners the full-ripened grain;
When I behold, upon the night's starred face,
   Huge cloudy symbols of a high romance,
And think that I may never live to trace
   Their shadows, with the magic hand of chance;
And when I feel, fair creature of an hour,
   That I shall never look upon thee more,
Never have relish in the faery power
   Of unreflecting love!—then on the shore
Of the wide world I stand alone, and think
Till Love and Fame to nothingness do sink.

BRIGHT STAR

Bright star, would I were steadfast as thou art—
   Not in lone splendor hung aloft the night
And watching, with eternal lids apart,
   Like nature's patient, sleepless Eremite,
The moving waters at their priestlike task
   Of pure ablution round earth's human shores,
Or gazing on the new soft fallen mask
   Of snow upon the mountains and the moors—
No—yet still steadfast, still unchangeable,
   Pillowed upon my fair love's ripening breast,
To feel forever its soft fall and swell,
   Awake forever in a sweet unrest,
Still, still to hear her tender-taken breath,
And so live ever—or else swoon to death.

LA BELLE DAME SANS MERCI

O what can ail thee, Knight at arms,
   Alone and palely loitering?
The sedge has withered from the Lake
   And no birds sing!

O what can ail thee, Knight at arms,
   So haggard, and so woebegone?
The squirrel's granary is full
   And the harvest's done.

I see a lily on thy brow
   With anguish moist and fever dew,
And on thy cheeks a fading rose
   Fast withereth too.

I met a Lady in the Meads,
   Full beautiful, a faery's child,
Her hair was long, her foot was light
   And her eyes were wild.

I made a Garland for her head,
   And bracelets too, and fragrant Zone;
She looked at me as she did love
   And made sweet moan.

I set her on my pacing steed
   And nothing else saw all day long,
For sidelong would she bend and sing
   A faery's song.

She found me roots of relish sweet,
   And honey wild, and manna dew,
And sure in language strange she said
   "I love thee true."

She took me to her elfin grot
   And there she wept and sighed full sore,
And there I shut her wild wild eyes
   With kisses four.

And there she lulléd me asleep,
   And there I dreamed, Ah Woe betide!
The latest dream I ever dreamt
   On the cold hill side.

I saw pale Kings, and Princes too,
   Pale warriors, death-pale were they all;
They cried, "La belle dame sans merci
   Thee hath in thrall!"

I saw their starved lips in the gloam
   With horrid warning gapéd wide,

And I awoke, and found me here
   On the cold hill's side.

And this is why I sojourn here,
   Alone and palely loitering;
Though the sedge is withered from the Lake
   And no birds sing.

TO AUTUMN

1

Season of mists and mellow fruitfulness,
   Close bosom-friend of the maturing sun;
Conspiring with him how to load and bless
   With fruit the vines that round the thatch-eaves run;
To bend with apples the mossed cottage-trees,
   And fill all fruit with ripeness to the core;
     To swell the gourd, and plump the hazel shells
   With a sweet kernel; to set budding more,
And still more, later flowers for the bees,
Until they think warm days will never cease,
     For Summer has o'er-brimmed their clammy cells.

2

Who hath not seen thee oft amid thy store?
   Sometimes whoever seeks abroad may find
Thee sitting careless on a granary floor,

Thy hair soft-lifted by the winnowing wind;
Or on a half-reaped furrow sound asleep,
   Drowsed with the fume of poppies, while thy hook
     Spares the next swath and all its twinéd flowers:
And sometimes like a gleaner thou dost keep
   Steady thy laden head across a brook;
   Or by a cider-press, with patient look,
     Thou watchest the last oozings hours by hours.

3

Where are the songs of Spring? Aye, where are they?
   Think not of them, thou hast thy music too—
While barred clouds bloom the soft-dying day,
   And touch the stubble-plains with rosy hue;
Then in a wailful choir the small gnats mourn
   Among the river sallows, borne aloft
     Or sinking as the light wind lives or dies;
And full-grown lambs loud bleat from hilly bourn;
   Hedge crickets sing; and now with treble soft
   The redbreast whistles from a garden croft;
     And gathering swallows twitter in the skies.

OZYMANDIAS

by Percy Bysshe Shelley

I met a traveller from an antique land,
Who said—"Two vast and trunkless legs of stone
Stand in the desert. . . . Near them, on the sand,
Half sunk a shattered visage lies, whose frown,
And wrinkled lip, and sneer of cold command,
Tell that its sculptor well those passions read
Which yet survive, stamped on these lifeless things,
The hand that mocked them, and the heart that fed;
And on the pedestal, these words appear:
My name is Ozymandias, King of Kings,
Look on my Works, ye Mighty, and despair!
Nothing beside remains. Round the decay
Of that colossal Wreck, boundless and bare
The lone and level sands stretch far away."

from ADONAIS

by Percy Bysshe Shelley

6

But now, thy youngest, dearest one, has perished
The nursling of thy widowhood, who grew,
Like a pale flower by some sad maiden cherished,
And fed with true love tears, instead of dew;
Most musical of mourners, weep anew!
Thy extreme hope, the loveliest and the last,
The bloom, whose petals nipt before they blew
Died on the promise of the fruit, is waste;
The broken lily lies—the storm is overpast.

42

He is made one with Nature: there is heard
His voice in all her music, from the moan
Of thunder, to the song of night's sweet bird;
He is a presence to be felt and known
In darkness and in light, from herb and stone,
Spreading itself where'er that Power may move
Which has withdrawn his being to its own;
Which wields the world with never wearied love,
Sustains it from beneath, and kindles it above.

Allegra Byron

DEAD BABIES

"Wail, For the World's Wrong"

*W*hile John Keats gushed out the last of his great poetry just before his final illness struck, both Shelley and Byron were living in Italy, though not necessarily always close to each other.

Since his self-imposed exile began, Byron had been moving from city to city—Rome, Venice, Genoa, Ravenna—back and forth. He always installed himself in grand style: His homes were huge, full of servants and animals, attractive young boys, and fiery mistresses. (One of his female lovers jumped into the Grand Canal in Venice when he dumped her. Another went on violent rampages, threatening him with a knife—which was probably sharper than Caro Lamb's had been a few years earlier.) He still thought about England, but there was little chance he would ever see his native land again.

His wife, Annabella (yes, they were still very much married), had gotten in touch with his half-sister, Augusta. Gradually, the Princess of Parallelograms began to turn the incestuous sister against her own flesh and blood, the brother who still wrote her love letters. Before long, both women were denouncing the sexual tastes of the infamous Lord Byron to anyone who would listen. And, this being juicy gossip, word spread. On a street in Rome, an English woman shielded the eyes of her teenage daughter when Byron passed by. "Don't look at him," she cautioned the innocent girl. "He is dangerous to look at." That was from a stranger—but even his friend Shelley told people that Byron was "as mad as the winds."

He was also getting scandalous to read. For years he'd been writing installments of a light, conversational poem about a fictional character whose sexual conquests were as famous as his own: Don Giovanni, or Don Juan. (When Byron talked with friends about the poem, he called his character Donny Johnny. And he pronounced Juan "Jew-wan," not "Hwan." It made for better rhyming.) Byron had left England during the age of the licentious Prince Regent. Anything went. But times and tastes and morals were changing, becoming more conservative. The Victorian Age wasn't that far in the future. And so the continuing tales of the scandalous Don were more a guilty pleasure than a blockbuster hit for Byron's readers back home. The publisher of the poem refused to put his name on the books—and he left off Byron's name, too. But there was no question who the author was. No one else would dare something like the cantos, or chapters, of *Don Juan*. The poem also made nasty remarks about the Romantic poets back in England, "the Lakers," as Byron referred to Wordsworth and Southey. Keats he called "Tadpole of the Lakes." (Byron never really counted himself as one of the Romantics. But the brooding, star-crossed heroes of his works were the ultimate in Romantic men.) Wordsworth shot back that the *Don Juan* serial "will do more harm to the English character, than anything of our time." Southey accused Byron of leading a "Satanic school" of poetry. Byron retorted, "The reading or non-reading a book will never keep down a single petticoat."

Alba, the product of the brief affair between Lord Byron and Claire Clairmont, was just a year and a half old when she left her mother, and England, in the company of Percy and Mary Shelley and young Willmouse, bound for Italy and one of her father's sprawling villas. With him, she lived as part of the menagerie that roamed freely through the mazelike halls, an intelligent, dark-haired, blue-eyed child among the bevy of beasts, a little Eve in a fallen Garden of Eden. Her companions were an eagle, a falcon, a tame crow, an Egyptian crane, peacocks, guinea hens, three monkeys, five cats, eight dogs, ten horses, and some geese Byron had been fattening for a feast but had grown too fond of to slaughter. They followed their master around the house like puppies. Besides a new country, a new home, and a new environment, Alba also received a new name. Byron insisted on calling the child whom he was still not sure was really his daughter, Clara Allegra Biron—to friends and family, just Allegra. Shelley would try to visit occasionally. But between being an obsessive-compulsive and a hypochondriac, he had a hard time dealing with the disarray of the Byron household. The women, he complained, "smell so of garlick." The pretty young boys and signs of homo- and bisexualty weren't to his tastes either, kinky as those could be.

One new constant *was* taking shape in Byron's wild life, however. His latest mistress was a petite brunette teenager, fresh out of a convent school and married to an elderly Italian count. Byron described Teresa Guiccioli as "a sort of an Italian Caroline Lamb," fiery and temperamental and very good at getting what she wanted. (To Shelley, who offered to help her learn English, she was "a very pretty sentimental innocent, superficial Italian." He'd originally added *stupid* to the list of adjectives, but crossed it out.) The man who had boasted that he'd had sex with more than two hundred women since his arrival in Venice had met his "last attachment." Once the scenes and the screaming were over, Countess Guiccioli was living with Byron, and not her aged and noble-born husband.

Now that they'd dropped Allegra off with Lord Byron, the Shelleys took up the same kind of life they'd led in England, just in a warmer climate. In Italy they were constantly on the move: Venice, Pisa, Naples, Florence, Rome. In the space of two years, they lived in eight different places. The moves weren't always happily motivated. In one city, Shelley was at the post office minding his own business, just picking up his mail. A complete stranger heard him say his name, walked over, screamed "Atheist!" and knocked him cold. The Shelleys quickly found a new address—and a different post office.

In Rome they did what all tourists do—strolled in the evening through the Pantheon, the Colosseum, the Forum, the ancient baths, viewed the art and sculpture Joseph Severn thought he was going to see when he signed on as Keats's traveling companion. Both Shelley and Mary were devout atheists, but they were introduced to the pope and even attended a Mass at St. Peter's—and they restrained themselves from making nasty, provocative comments, as they'd done during so many church services in England. They found the Roman Catholic rituals entertaining and attractive, in an artistic, theatrical sort of way.

For Shelley, Italy was an inspiration. He was writing long, politically subversive poems; working on a lurid play with a theme of incest that no theater dared perform; and contemplating his first gray hairs in "Ode to the West Wind." He stopped worrying about consumption and insisted that Italy's warm weather was just what John Keats had needed to cure what ailed him.

For Mary, however, those years in Italy were more a hell than a heaven.

First they received word that, in Byron's home in Venice, Allegra was ill. Claire demanded to see her child. Both Shelley and his infant daughter, Clara, had a touch of the fever, but he agreed to move the whole family so Claire could be reunited with Byron and their girl. Whatever had been wrong with Allegra, it wasn't serious. Claire and Byron had some good long talks. But they never sat down or played with Allegra as a family. It was always one parent or the other, as they'd agreed. If Claire was hoping for reconciliation, it didn't happen. The Shelleys, however, paid the heaviest price for the trip. Little Clara Shelley's fever was worsening. It wasn't until she went into convulsions that Shelley tried to get her to a doctor. But it was too late; Clara died.

In June of 1819, William Shelley—Willmouse, the family's favorite—also came down with a fever. A few days later, the beloved four-year-old, too, was dead.

Babies in the 1800s were much, much less likely to live to adulthood than they are today—just as mothers were less likely to survive to raise their babies. That didn't mean that mothers were ever prepared for the loss. Mary was growing more and more depressed. Shelley kept her almost constantly pregnant, but after so many pregnancies, they didn't have a single surviving child to show for it. To keep her occupied, Shelley—and sometimes Byron—gave Mary the usual job reserved for writers' wives and mistresses: fair copyist. There were no such things as Wite-Out or computers to correct errors, of course. Poets took up a pen, dashed off their work, edited right on the page, and went on to the next project. They couldn't be bothered with turning a manuscript full of cross-outs, corrections, arrows, and tiny notes in margins into something a publisher could make sense of and print as the author would want it. That was what fair copyists were for. They were usually people who knew the writer well enough to have a good idea what all those cross-outs, corrections, arrows, and notes meant, so they didn't have to keep asking questions of the artist at work. Copying the works of two prolific poets kept Mary busy, but the loss of her babies was always on her mind.

Meanwhile, Byron had finally come to realize that a house full of animals, temperamental mistresses, and pretty boys might not be the best environment for a growing girl. Teresa Guiccioli had some family connections that helped Byron get Allegra into a convent school. She arrived there like a tiny princess, arms loaded with toys and dolls, her outfit made from the robes her father had once worn to sit in Parliament. She thought the nuns were her servants. It was the first time in her life she had had other children to play with. When Byron visited, Allegra endured his company just long enough to get her hands on the gingerbread he always brought.

Those devout atheists, the Shelleys, and especially Claire, couldn't deal with the fact that their little Allegra was being raised, not just surrounded by religion, but by Catholics—*Papists*. (Years earlier, Sir Walter Scott had met Byron. There was something about the irreverent young lord that made the old poet laureate predict that he'd die a Catholic. Byron himself was attracted to the religion: "It is by far the most elegant worship, hardly excepting the Greek mythology. What with incense, pictures, statues, altars, shrines, relics, and the real presence, confession, absolution,—there is something sensible to grasp at. Besides, it leaves no possibility of doubt; for those who swallow their Deity, really and truly, in transubstantiation, can hardly find any thing else otherwise than easy of digestion.") The Shelleys offered at one point to take Allegra into their own home. Byron, very aware of their dismal track record at keeping babies alive, was not about to trust them with his daughter. "Have they *reared* one?" he quipped cruelly—but accurately.

Claire was not allowed to see Allegra in the convent. She began to have premonitions that there was something wrong, that her daughter was ill, was dying, needed her. She begged Byron for a chance to visit the little girl. He refused. If she had to, Claire told Mary, she would kidnap Allegra—there had to be a way.

Like a diabolical version of Wordsworth, Shelley had a knack for gathering people around him who shared his views on life. In Italy, he was a magnet for Englishmen—and women—with radical outlooks, and often radical lifestyles. He considered founding a sort of English artists' colony in Pisa. Sometimes Byron was in residence, in a house his valet, Fletcher, insisted was haunted. Leigh Hunt, his wife, and their brood of eleven children joined Shelley, too. (Hunt's little ones enjoyed drawing on Shelley's walls, which did not endear them to the poet. They tried doing the same thing at Byron's house, but his bulldog was trained to growl at them on sight.) Also part of the group were Edward and Jane Williams, who shared a last name simply as a formality; they were just living together. Another friend, Edward Trelawny, was, said Byron, "the personification of my Corsair," with his dark good looks and his pirate's taste in clothing—flowing, open-necked blouses and bandannas. Then there was a Greek noble-man, Prince Mavrocordato, who told his English friends of the troubles in his country, the struggle to be free from Turkish rule.

Soon the Shelley party was involved in its usual distraction from any crisis: moving. There had been an ugly incident of horse-back road rage between one of their English friends and an Italian army officer in Pisa, resulting in bad blood. They were being pressured to leave. Quickly. Shelley and Edward Williams had found a house in Lerici, a fishing village on the Gulf of Spezia, that would be perfect for a summer on the water. They were in the middle of packing when word came that Claire's worst premonitions had been a mother's intuition: Allegra had come down with typhus. She'd died in the convent on April 19, 1822.

The Shelleys decided it would be best not to break the bad news to Claire right away—they'd find the right moment. She could get very emotional, and this wasn't a good time. But there were whispered conversations during the packing and strange, sad looks in her direction. She confronted Shelley with the question, and he couldn't deny it. All Claire requested from Byron, through Shelley, were a miniature portrait of their daughter and a lock of her hair as keepsakes.

Allegra's body was sent back to England for burial—but not in a churchyard. Her father's reputation had tainted even the innocent. Not only was she illegitimate, she was *Lord Byron's* brat.

Such a short time ago, life had seemed so pleasant and care-free for the friends and their young families. The warm Italian sun shone down on them, words poured eloquently from their pens, their children played happily in their spacious villas. It had been too good to last.

The Poems

ODE TO THE WEST WIND

by Percy Bysshe Shelley

O wild West Wind, thou breath of Autumn's being,
Thou, from whose unseen presence the leaves dead
Are driven, like ghosts from an enchanter fleeing,

Yellow, and black, and pale, and hectic red,
Pestilence-stricken multitudes: O Thou,
Who chariotest to their dark wintry bed

The winged seeds, where they lie cold and low,
Each like a corpse within its grave, until
Thine azure sister of the Spring shall blow

Her clarion o'er the dreaming earth, and fill
(Driving sweet buds like flocks to feed in air)
With living hues and odours plain and hill:

Wild Spirit, which art moving everywhere;
Destroyer and Preserver; hear, O hear!

II

Thou on whose stream, 'mid the steep sky's commotion,

Loose clouds like Earth's decaying leaves are shed,

Shook from the tangled boughs of Heaven and Ocean,

Angels of rain and lightning: there are spread

On the blue surface of thine aery surge,

Like the bright hair uplifted from the head

Of some fierce Maenad, even from the dim verge

Of the horizon to the zenith's height,

The locks of the approaching storm. Thou Dirge

Of the dying year, to which this closing night

Will be the dome of a vast sepulchre,

Vaulted with all thy congregated might

Of vapours, from whose solid atmosphere

Black rain and fire and hail will burst: O hear!

III

Thou who didst waken from his summer dreams

The blue Mediterranean, where he lay,

Lulled by the coil of his chrystalline streams,

Beside a pumice isle in Baiae's bay,

And saw in sleep old palaces and towers

Quivering within the wave's intenser day,

All overgrown with azure moss and flowers
So sweet, the sense faints picturing them! Thou
For whose path the Atlantic's level powers

Cleave themselves into chasms, while far below
The sea-blooms and the oozy woods which wear
The sapless foliage of the ocean, know

Thy voice, and suddenly grow grey with fear,
And tremble and despoil themselves: O hear!

IV

If I were a dead leaf thou mightest bear;
If I were a swift cloud to fly with thee;
A wave to pant beneath thy power, and share

The impulse of thy strength, only less free
Than thou, O Uncontrollable! If even
I were as in my boyhood, and could be

The comrade of thy wanderings over Heaven,
As then, when to outstrip thy skiey speed
Scarce seemed a vision; I would ne'er have striven

As thus with thee in prayer in my sore need.
Oh! lift me as a wave, a leaf, a cloud!
I fall upon the thorns of life! I bleed!

A heavy weight of hours has chained and bowed
One too like thee: tameless, and swift, and proud.

V

Make me thy lyre, even as the forest is:
What if my leaves are falling like its own!
The tumult of thy mighty harmonies

Will take from both a deep, autumnal tone,
Sweet though in sadness. Be thou, Spirit fierce,
My spirit! Be thou me, impetuous one!

Drive my dead thoughts over the universe
Like withered leaves to quicken a new birth!
And, by the incantation of this verse,

Scatter, as from an unextinguished hearth
Ashes and sparks, my words among mankind!
Be through my lips to unawakened Earth

The trumpet of a prophecy! O Wind,
If Winter comes, can Spring be far behind?

TO JANE (THE KEEN STARS WERE TWINKLING)
by Percy Bysshe Shelley

The keen stars were twinkling
And the fair moon was rising among them,
    Dear Jane.
    The guitar was tinkling
But the notes were not sweet 'till you sung them
    Again.—
    As the moon's soft splendour
O'er the faint cold starlight of Heaven
    Is thrown—
    So your voice most tender
To the strings without soul had then given
    Its own.

The stars will awaken,
Though the moon sleep a full hour later,
    Tonight;
    No leaf will be shaken
While the dews of your melody scatter
    Delight.
    Though the sound overpowers
Sing again, with your dear voice revealing
    A tone
    Of some world far from ours,

Where music and moonlight and feeling
    Are one.

A Dirge

by Percy Bysshe Shelley

Rough wind, that moanest loud
  Grief too sad for song;
Wild wind, when sullen cloud
  Knells all the night long;
Sad storm, whose tears are vain,
Bare woods, whose branches strain,
Deep caves and dreary main,—
  Wail, for the world's wrong!

The Funeral of Shelley

Dead Poets

"So We'll Go No More A-Roving"

$\mathcal{S}$helley was obsessed with water—and drowning. A fortune-teller Lord Byron once consulted told him to beware his thirty-seventh year. So perhaps, on some subconscious level, they each knew what was coming.

One thing Shelley and Edward Williams had in common was a love of sailing. They'd taken a little boat out a few times together. It was scary how often they made it to harbor just as a storm was rolling in, but they'd been lucky. Now that they had the house in Lerici, they decided to invest in a boat of their own.

The Casa Magni in Lerici had started its life as a boathouse, which was why it was so close to the water. The stone floors were never without a thin coating of sand, tracked in by people walking, blown in by the wind off the Gulf of Spezia. But the two

couples, two children, and a contingent of servants made themselves at home in a house haunted by the constant sound of waves.

The sound of waves wasn't all that was haunting Shelley.
Ever since Allegra's death, he'd been having strange dreams,
terrible nightmares of a dead child, her long hair dripping, her
pale body draped in seaweed, staggering out of the sea. Even
awake, he wasn't safe from horrible visions. And his hallucinations were bloody and violent. He imagined his hands around
Mary's neck, squeezing harder, harder; the bodies of Edward
and Jane Williams lying torn to pieces on the sandy bloodstained
stone floor of Casa Magni.

Some of the bloodiest incidents were not hallucinations but
reality. When the Shelleys moved into Casa Magni, Mary was—
as usual—pregnant. Suddenly she doubled over in pain and felt a
flow of blood that shouldn't be. She had suffered a miscarriage.
And there was so much blood. . . . Shelley sent for a doctor, but
he was afraid Mary would die from loss of blood before help
could arrive. He hurried to the nearby icehouse, filled a tub, and
lowered Mary, now barely conscious, into the freezing water. It
staunched the hemorrhage and saved her life.

So it looked like a welcome distraction when the boat Shelley and Williams had ordered finally arrived. And she was a
beauty, sailing into the Gulf of Spezia on May 12, 1822, on the
wings of a storm: twenty-four feet long, with two mainmasts
and plenty of sails. Unfortunately, one of those sails was painted
with the name of the new boat: *Don Juan*. Shelley was uncomfortable with a name that would constantly remind him of

Byron, whom he considered his only real rival as a poet. He tried to paint over the name, but the letters kept bleeding through. Finally he had to cut the offending bit of canvas away and sew a clean patch over it. The *Don Juan* was rechristened *Ariel*.

Back in England, Byron's mother-in-law—Annabella Milbanke's mother—died. Since the couple was not legally divorced, part of the inheritance she left belonged to him—a very nice amount. A month after Shelley took possession of the *Ariel*, Edward Trelawny sailed Byron's brand-new boat, the *Bolivar*, into the harbor at Livorno, firing off a six-gun salute. She was a magnificent schooner boasting velvet-covered seats, genuine Italian marble in her bathrooms, and two cannons. Like the coach Byron had had built for his journey from England to Italy, she turned heads wherever she went.

Shelley and Edward Williams sailed the *Ariel* from Lerici to Livorno to admire Byron's *Bolivar*. As their visit came to a close, Edward Trelawny said he wanted to go back to Lerici on the *Ariel*. The time came to sail and Trelawny hadn't arrived, so Shelley and Williams, along with a young assistant named Charles Vivian, set off on their own. It was about two o'clock in the afternoon on July 8, 1822, and there had been violent thunderstorms nearly every afternoon that summer; another seemed to be building. The storm struck around six thirty, when the *Ariel* was already far from shore. The crew of a fishing boat that saw her reported that she was struggling before the gale with all her magnificent sails flying. They offered to help Shelley, Williams, and Vivian, who were obviously in trouble. Shelley said they didn't need assistance. So the fishing crew advised them to at least furl the sails, to give the raging wind less to play with. Williams started to do so. Shelley made him stop. Then, fearing for their own safety, the men on the fishing boat moved on until the *Ariel* was out of sight behind the waves and the driving rain.

For ten days, Mary Shelley, Jane Williams, Trelawny, and Byron watched the sea and waited for word from the *Ariel*. It was still possible, they supposed, that the boat had made it to some distant harbor, its crew alive but unable to get a message to their loved ones. But hope dwindled with every day that passed.

Then, on July 18, the little group heard that some bodies had washed ashore on the beach at Via Reggio. Faceless, armless, they'd obviously been in the water for some time. Byron and Trelawny went to investigate. Trousers and a jacket that looked like Shelley's were still hanging from one bloated torso. Then the men searched through the pockets—and found a waterlogged copy of Keats's *Lamia,* folded and crushed as if its owner had been reading it until the moment he'd needed to stash it away very suddenly. There was no longer any doubt. Percy Bysshe Shelley, Edward Williams, and Charles Vivian had drowned in the last sailing of the *Ariel*.

Italy was very disease-conscious. It required bodies that washed ashore to be covered with quicklime to speed decomposition, then buried right there on the beach. For their friend Shelley, however, Byron and company had other ideas. After Shelley's remains had lain beneath the sand for nearly a month, a small party of Englishmen arrived on the forlorn beach. Between them they dragged a small iron furnace, courtesy of Edward Trelawny. Gagging into their handkerchiefs, they dug up the grave and exhumed their friend's unrecognizable body, then stuffed what was left of it into the furnace. For hours, the corpse burned as the friends tossed handfuls of incense, salt, sugar, and wine into the flames. Byron, sunburned from a swim out to the *Bolivar* to while away the three hours it took for his friend's body to burn, wanted to retrieve Shelley's skull from the fire while it was still intact, but Trelawny held him back. He'd heard the stories of young Byron at Newstead Abbey and the midnight parties when he'd drunk wine from a monk's skull.

When nearly all that was left in the furnace was ashes, the macabre ceremony was over. Shelley's cremated remains were shoveled into a mahogany box, which ended up spending several months in the British consul's wine cellar. Eventually the box was buried in Rome's Protestant Cemetery, not far from Shelley's friend and fellow poet—the last poet he'd read in this life, John Keats. Shelley's heart had been found, nearly unburnt, in the middle of the ashes, a solid, charred lump. The men placed it in a small casket and gave it to Mary. When she finally returned to England, she had it buried in the churchyard in Bournemouth.

Shelley was just thirty when he died. Mary, twenty-five, was a widow with an infant son, Percy—destined to become the only Shelley to survive beyond childhood. Mary was still able to collect some money each year from Shelley's inheritance. She wanted very much to write a biography of her husband—since she *was* an accomplished writer—but his family had the final say. If she wished, Mary could have editions of Shelley's poems published, and she could add her own footnotes and explanations in the margins. But a real biography would need to wait until Sir Timothy, her father-in-law, was himself dead. After all, he had to protect the family name. If Mary disobeyed, he would discontinue her annuity. Once again, Byron tried to take Mary's mind off her difficulties by giving her work to do, fair copying his poems.

Byron was preoccupied lately, and this time not (much) with Teresa Guiccioli. He'd been reminded of a cause that had been close to his heart since that first trip just out of university, when he'd promised himself that one day Greece would be free from Turkish rule. It—philhellenism—was a cause other Englishmen shared; even Shelley had written a poem on the sad state of affairs in the country that had introduced democracy to the world. Now, banished from his own country, floating free in Italy, Byron had been recruited by the London Greek Committee to advise them on how to assist the Greek independence movement. Because of Teresa, he'd once considered becoming part of the Italian revolutionary movement, the Carbonari, in which her father and brother were both active. But Byron didn't foresee Italy breaking away from Austria in the near future. The Greece he'd fallen in love with as a young man, on the other hand, called to him now that his hair was graying. He agreed to fund the purchase of equipment and arms, sail to Greece, and then organize troops, perhaps as many as three thousand men.

Always the showman, Byron ordered gaudy, scarlet-and-gold uniforms for the soldiers under his command. They included plumed helmets, like something out of Homer's epics, which gave Edward Trelawny a good laugh. Byron secured a 120-ton brigantine, the *Hercules,* which he loaded with medical supplies and a doctor, Francesco Bruno, a young man who had just completed his studies. With him, Byron brought two of his dogs, Moretto the bulldog and Lyon the Newfoundland; the faithful valet Fletcher; several horses; and a black groom, Benjamin Lewis, to care for them.

Byron's mission was to lead an attack on Lepanto on the Gulf of Corinth. He was told that the most strategic place to set up camp was at Missolonghi. The town was low, swampy, wet and rainy, and infested with mosquitoes that bred malaria. The conditions would have been irrelevant if the troops had been satisfactory—but Byron was quickly disillusioned. The Greek soldiers were no more organized than the Italian revolutionaries he'd mocked not long ago. Some were mercenaries who would fight for whichever side paid them best. Others were fighting for their own region or clan, not for the independence of the country of Greece. The master of artillery assigned to Byron had no idea how to operate the sort of guns his troops had been sent. On the brighter side, many of the young English soldiers would gladly recite whole passages of his poems by heart—generally the bawdy ones—when they learned that Lord Byron himself was among their leaders.

To get away from the squalor and disorganization of the camp, Byron would take one of his horses and go riding in the countryside, regardless of the weather. But these were not the sunny Greek mountains he'd visited as a young man—and at thirty-seven, he was no longer a young man. Like many of the men forced to live in the swamp, he began to feel sick. In February of 1824, he collapsed with a seizure of some sort, perhaps a stroke, perhaps the onset of fever, or perhaps simply exhaustion. At the time, doctors explained away fevers as an excess of blood in the body. The cure? Bleeding, either by cutting or by the application of bloodsucking leeches, which was exactly what the inexperienced Dr. Bruno prescribed. Byron didn't have a much more sensible explanation for his illness. He sent a man out to comb the countryside, looking for the witch who had cursed him with the evil eye. Hadn't there just been an earthquake? It had to be a curse of some kind. The poet's one comfort during his recuperation was affectionate Lyon, the huge Newfoundland.

April 9 looked like it might be a fair day. Byron was still feeling under the weather, but he had to get out of that depressing camp and away from blood-happy Dr. Bruno. Benjamin Lewis saddled one of the horses, and Byron set out. When the inevitable pouring rain began to fall, it was a long way back to Missolonghi. By the time Byron returned, soaked to the skin, he was aching and feverish. A week later, he was so sick Dr. Bruno wasn't sure he could do much more to help him. He advised getting him to a more experienced physician, but the weather had turned so stormy it was impossible to move him. In the meantime, Bruno tried again and again to bleed Byron. But Byron was adamant: He wouldn't let the bloodsucker near him.

On April 16, Byron said, "I want to sleep now," closed his

eyes, and lapsed into a coma. Bruno took advantage of his patient's unconsciousness and slipped eight live leeches from their container in his medical kit. He placed them on Byron's forehead, and they began to do their work, sucking out the patient's fevered blood.

Around six in the afternoon on April 19—exactly two years since Allegra Biron had died in an Italian convent—a violent thunderstorm struck. As lightning bolts split the darkened sky asunder and thunderclaps shook the ground like lesser earthquakes, Fletcher the faithful valet went to check on his master, who had been unconscious now for three days. He found Byron dead.

Byron had left very specific instructions in case of his death. He did not want his body autopsied, and he wished to be buried in Greece: "I am sure my bones would not rest in an English grave, or my clay mix with the earth of that country. I believe the thought would drive me mad on my death-bed could I suppose that any of my friends would be base enough to convey my carcass back to her soil. I would not even feed her worms if I could help it."

But there was nothing a dead man could do to get his way. A doctor cut the corpse open to examine the organs—a liver deteriorated from years of dissolute living; a heart damaged by a lifetime of ballooning and plummeting weight, bingeing and purging; fused bones like an old man's. Edward Trelawny insisted on touching his friend's clubfoot, an invasion of privacy Byron would never have permitted in life. Only a small part of Byron was indeed left in Greek soil: his heart. The rest of him was packed into a wooden coffin and shipped off to England.

Byron was finally repeating a trip he'd made many years earlier as a fiery young lord. He was going home at last. But in those days before refrigeration was invented, there was a danger that his body would decompose before it reached its destination. So the coffin was submerged in a tub of alcohol to preserve it. The trip took three months. The alcohol didn't work very well. In London, the coffin was opened so the body could be positively identified. Byron's old school friend Hobhouse studied what was left of the corpse and wasn't sure who he was looking at, until he saw Byron's right foot.

Byron's reputation continued to haunt him even after he was dead. Since he *had* been one of England's major poets, there was a suggestion made to bury him inside Westminster Abbey, the huge church in London into whose crypts and side altars and under whose massive flooring stones important Englishmen went to eternal glory and recognition after they'd died. The request was refused. Yes, Byron had been an incredible talent, but he'd simply been too notorious for that kind of honor. So, said Hobhouse, he'd be "buried like a nobleman—since we could not bury him like a poet." Forty-seven carriages representing England's finest families escorted Lord Byron's body from London to Hucknall Torkard, not far from his old home of Newstead Abbey. But most of them were empty. Byron's peers just couldn't bring themselves to show their faces at the funeral of a man they'd spent so many years spreading scandal about—

but it would be poor etiquette *not* to show their respects, either. Among those noticeably absent from the funeral was Byron's half-sister and ex-lover, Augusta.

As if he was sure he'd be even more famous after his death than he'd been in his lifetime, Byron had been writing his memoirs. He'd given the manuscript to Hobhouse with the understanding that it could be published after he died. Everyone knew that Byron had lived a colorful life, but in the autobiography, nothing was omitted. Even Hobhouse, who'd been part of some of the escapades, was scandalized as he read the pages. Then Annabella and Augusta—the two women who had the most to lose if the whole, ugly truth were revealed—got wind of Byron's last bit of writing. They had their representatives look at the memoirs. Everyone agreed. For the sake of his own already soiled reputation and the reputation of his female family members, Byron's autobiography must be burnt.

In just three years, England's Romantic movement had lost three of its most influential poets. But the originals were still around.

The Poems

So We'll Go No More A-Roving
by George Gordon, Lord Byron

1

So we'll go no more a-roving
   So late into the night,
Though the heart be still as loving,
   And the moon be still as bright.

2

For the sword outwears its sheath,
   And the soul wears out the breast,
And the heart must pause to breathe,
   And Love itself have rest.

3

Though the night was made for loving,
   And the day returns too soon,
Yet we'll go no more a-roving
   By the light of the moon.

MEMORY (DRAFT VERSION)

by Percy Bysshe Shelley

Rose leaves, when the rose is dead,
Are heaped for the beloved's bed,
And so thy thoughts, when thou art gone,
Love itself shall slumber on. . . .

Music, when soft voices die,
Vibrates in the memory.—
Odours, when sweet violets sicken,
Live within the sense they quicken.—

WHEN A MAN HATH NO FREEDOM TO FIGHT FOR AT HOME

by George Gordon, Lord Byron

When a man hath no freedom to fight for at home,
    Let him combat for that of his neighbors;
Let him think of the glories of Greece and of Rome,
    And get knocked on his head for his labors.

To do good to mankind is the chivalrous plan,
    And is always as nobly requited;
Then battle for freedom wherever you can,
    And, if not shot or hanged, you'll get knighted.

Robert Southey

Lives Touched

"Old, Unhappy, Far-Off Things"

*S*amuel Taylor Coleridge huddled in his drug dealer's doorway to watch as Lord Byron's funeral procession moved slowly through the London streets. He was putting up a convincing front that he had kicked his opium habit, but since his days as cavalryman Silas T. Comberbache, he'd been a credible actor. He had a hushed understanding with one city pharmacist: He'd arrive surreptitiously at a secluded side entrance to the shop, never by the front door. Money would change hands, and he'd be slipped his supply of opium, no one the wiser.

It had been a long, hard climb back to something like a normal life for Coleridge. Now one of the men who'd been a huge help to him was gone. Gone, too, was Keats, who had seemed too young to be walking so intimately with death when the two

Edith Southey

men met on Hampstead Heath.

It had all begun so hopefully, the Romantic ideal that William Wordsworth and Samuel Taylor Coleridge had spun as young, rebellious poets. The poetry had caught on, with its everyday language, its ordinary characters, its delicious imagery, its hallmark of deep emotion. But the people who had invested their lives in establishing that poetry now seemed to have gotten very little pleasure out of it, and the lives that touched theirs were no happier.

Nine children of three sets of parents grew up at Greta Hall, the rambling house in Keswick that Robert Southey had taken over from his old friend Coleridge. Greta Hall's many residents jokingly called it the Aunt Hill—the Anthill. The nickname had a double meaning: It was always swarming with people, *and* it was full of "aunts." There were Robert Southey; his wife, Edith (a Fricker sister), and their four surviving children; the widowed Mary (Fricker) Lovell and her son; and, after the separation, Sarah (Fricker) Coleridge and her daughter, Sara (and, occasionally, the Coleridge boys, too). Until Coleridge and Wordsworth had their falling out, the Aunt Hill swarm also included the young Wordsworths—John, Willie, and Dora. When Coleridge walked away from the Lakes for the last time without even stopping at the Wordsworth home to say good-bye, his children lost not only a full-time parent but a set of beloved playmates as well.

Greta Hall had a second nickname: Cat Eden. Through its halls prowled the resident felines: Pulcheria, Madame Bianchi, Lord Nelson, Bona Fidelia, Baron Chinchilla, Hurlyburlybuss, Archduchess Knurry-Murry-Purry-Hurry-Skurry, and Pope Joan (who had gone by the name Prester John until "he" was found nursing a litter of kittens).

Some of the more creative cat names were probably the doing of Mrs. Coleridge. She had a knack for making up silly words on the spur of the moment. Her fellow Aunt Hillers called her special language the Lingo Grande. When the children were being loud, for instance, the "childeroapusses [were] bangrampating about the house [all] rudderfish and roughcumtatherick." Boring visitors? "Drigdraggery stupossums." Maybe, considering the way she played with language, she was a better match for her poet husband than busybody Dorothy Wordsworth had once thought.

The adults tried their best to give the children a solid, happy home life. All the girls—along with Herbert Southey, who was sickly and unable to go to a boarding school like other boys his age—were taught at home, and their education was exemplary. There was always someone to play with, always a book to read or poetry being recited, always interesting conversation, because the children were living with Robert Southey, the man who'd been England's poet laureate since 1813, and with relatives of some of the country's greatest literary minds.

It was Sara, the one Coleridge child who was raised primarily by her mother rather than her father, who showed a spark of the poet's genius. But she was also the child he most ignored. When they both were small, before her father and Wordsworth had fallen out, she and Dora Wordsworth had played together, along with Edith May Southey. Coleridge had nothing but good things to say about Dora, the "beautiful Cat of the Mountains." Sara knew competition when she saw it. When asked if she thought Dora Wordsworth—Dora of the long, blond curls—was pretty, Sara responded no. Nothing Sara did seemed to make her father like her as much as he seemed to like Dora Wordsworth, even though Sara was smart, pretty, sensitive, and good with words. Her brother Hartley once called her "a visible soul." She retorted that he was "a visible fool" for saying something like that.

Hartley, the child who'd spent so much time in a fantasy world, had grown into a troubled teen. After attending Merton College at Oxford University, he got a position as a tutor at Oriel College there and was in line for a fellowship. Things had changed a bit since the last generation had attended university, especially at Oriel. Once undergraduates had spent their days sleeping and their nights partying; now they were expected to study—and so were their tutors. This wasn't in Hartley Coleridge's nature. He was drinking, carousing, keeping company with a wild and bohemian class of people not normally seen around staid Oriel. When his reputation got bad enough, he was kicked out. Like father, like son. Confronted with disgrace, Hartley disappeared off the face of the earth. Coleridge desperately followed a rumor that his son had been seen getting onto a ship in Liverpool, headed for the United States. Instead, he found the boy in London, in the care of incredibly patient, kindly Basil Montagu and family. But it didn't take long for them to give up on *another* Coleridge with a substance abuse problem. The Montagus eventually kicked Hartley out. Then, as his brothers had done for him when he was the Coleridge black sheep, Samuel tried to get Hartley reinstated at Oriel.

Samuel Coleridge was down on his luck, so friends pooled enough money to send Derwent, Hartley's younger brother, to university—this time, Cambridge. The good news was that Derwent lacked the worst of Hartley's problems. The bad news was that he lacked his troubled brother's intelligence as well. His nickname was Stumpy Canary. Derwent Coleridge's university life was uneventful; after graduating, he became a minister—one of the jobs his father had seriously considered as a young man but wasn't really cut out for. Derwent lived out his life as an unremarkable clergyman in the West Country, not far from where his father had grown up.

Back at Rydal Mount, the Wordsworths' home, the star among the children was—again—a daughter: the beautiful Dora. She was far brighter than either of her brothers. Willie lacked ambition. John had a learning disability, which nineteenth-century teachers

Edith Southey and Sara Coleridge

didn't understand or know how to deal with. To them, he was just stupid. It was Dora who went away to boarding school—against her wishes, since she saw her friends at Greta Hall being homeschooled in a far livelier environment. (With so much going on next door, Dora called her own home Idle Mount.) It was also Dora who showed the most spirit and fire, the kind her father had had in his younger, revolutionary days. She spent quite a bit of time locked in her room, grounded after throwing temper tantrums.

But the older poets didn't necessarily like the competition they saw emerging in the next generation. When William Wordsworth heard that Sara Coleridge showed some promise as a writer, he told her to be more like Edith May Southey: interested in fashions, hairstyles, *proper* girl things. Sara's mother assured her daughter that even girls could be writers. But in the same house, Robert Southey had opinions more along the lines of Wordsworth's. One day he received a letter and a writing sample from a young woman from Yorkshire by the name of C. (as in Charlotte) Brontë. He wrote back that she should concentrate on getting married instead. "Literature cannot be the business of a woman's life and it ought not to be." When you hear that sort of opinion often enough from people you respect, you start to believe it, whether or not it's true. Once C. Brontë overcame popular prejudice and created her masterpiece, Sara Coleridge insisted *Jane Eyre* was the work of a man.

A friendship as close as the one between William Wordsworth and Samuel Taylor Coleridge doesn't just die and stay dead. The two men were estranged for about fifteen years. Then they made some fitful stabs at reconciliation. But it was like an old love affair. The mutual passion and creativity that had bonded them in the first place weren't there anymore, and both men had been hurt badly by the other. They tried getting back together by drawing up a document with a mediator, getting all their disagreements and emotional wounds out in the open, in writing. But that seemed cold and soulless and didn't do what had been intended: restore a broken friendship. On the positive side, they *were* speaking. In 1828 they tried to bring back the old days with a trip to Germany, just the three with one soul, together again: Coleridge, William, Dorothy.

It was a time in his life when Coleridge was trying to set things right in his many relationships that had failed. In 1823 he had finally met his daughter again, after nearly seven years apart. Even he could no longer say that Sara wasn't as beautiful as Dora Wordsworth or as properly feminine as Edith May Southey. C. R. Leslie, a prominent American portrait painter, was in London, exhibiting a picture of Sara Coleridge in Scottish dress, looking like a Highland lass Wordsworth had described in one of his poems. She was not just pretty, she was breathtaking. On a visit to London around the time the portrait was unveiled, Sara was hailed by society as "Exquisite Sara—Flower of the Lakes" and the "Sylph of Ullswater." When she went to the theater, she stole the show; the audience clambered onto seats to get a better look at her.

She was bound to attract suitors, but not everyone in the family was happy when one actually caught her eye. One of her cousins, Henry Coleridge, was also in London, encouraging his famous poet uncle to talk and writing down the fascinating conversations they had together for a book he would call *Table Talk*. Henry met Sara during one of these oral history "recording sessions." It was love at first sight. His father and some Coleridge uncles tried to discourage the affair: Did young Henry really want to marry into the side of the family that might have a streak of insanity and definitely had problems with drug abuse? Henry was sent abroad in the hopes he'd forget his beautiful, brilliant cousin. Samuel happened to see one of his nephew's letters, gushing with adoration for his lovely Sara. From that time on, for what it was worth from a questionably sane old drug addict, he threw in his support for the young lovers. And in the end, true love prevailed. The cousins were married in 1829.

Hartley, meanwhile, went steadily downhill. He stopped in London one day to visit his father. Like most young men who suddenly drop out of the blue to visit their fathers, he said he needed money. Like most doting fathers with their oldest sons,

Coleridge gave him some. Hartley promised he'd see his father again soon. The next the family heard of him, he had run away to the Lake District. Theoretically, he was a teacher there. In reality, he spent most of his time at the Red Lion Inn in Grasmere, drinking himself into oblivion. Homeless, he wandered about the hills, occasionally spinning out a bit of poetry, even publishing one book of poems. He dedicated the volume to his father and sent him a copy. According to the Wordsworths, who would see the former playmate of their children staggering about Grasmere, the young man was suicidal.

As these Wordsworth, Coleridge, and Southey children grew up and started lives of their own, daily life for the adults left at the Aunt Hill and Rydal Mount, the Wordsworth home, was deteriorating. Child mortality was high at the time. Half the babies who were born died before reaching adulthood. Fevers, measles, pneumonia, dysentery, tuberculosis, all were potentially fatal before the wonders of twentieth-century medicine. The standard treatments and cures were still bleeding, opium, a warm climate, rest. The families at Rydal Mount and Greta Hall were not exceptions to these sad statistics. Sarah Coleridge had four babies, yet raised only three. Mary Wordsworth lost two of her five children. And Edith Southey, who bore eight babies, was left with only four children.

Depression, guilt that there was something she hadn't done—or *had* done—to deserve such losses, fear for the health of her remaining children, all weighed heavily and constantly on Edith's mind and took their toll. Her behavior grew increasingly unpredictable and disturbing. Robert finally sent her to a "retreat"—an asylum for the insane run by kindly Quakers, not far from the city of York. Edith Southey, who had married her Robert in the hopes of starting a new life in a utopian American pantisocracy, died in 1837.

Robert Southey quickly found a new wife, Caroline Bowles. They had known each other for a long time, and she was also a writer. But the new marriage didn't make it much past the honeymoon. Robert, already in his sixties, suffered a stroke. His memory as well as his health was affected; he had no idea who the woman was who sat by his bedside. He died in 1843.

Things weren't that different at Rydal Mount, but the invalid in this case was Dorothy. There were periods when she was confused about who she was, who the people around her were, where she was, yet at times she seemed perfectly normal. Her lucid episodes grew shorter and fewer and farther between as the months went by. Her symptoms seem like what we know today as Alzheimer's disease. Since she also had a variety of aches and pains and health complaints, her doctor was prescribing opium, which didn't help her confusion. Dorothy, the woman whose notebook entries had been nearly as lyrical as her famous brother's poems, the woman who had tramped in heavy hiking boots across the rolling fells of England and the icy slopes of the Alps alongside her beloved brother and his best friend, was confined to the top floor of Rydal Mount. There she would splash happily in a tub full of soapsuds and get her amusement from a gift a friend named Isabella Fenwick had given to William, a cuckoo clock. Sometimes the gates to the property would be locked so curious outsiders couldn't peek in (since tourists to the Lakes were always trying to get a glimpse of their favorite living poet), and a nurse would wheel Dorothy out into the garden in a makeshift wheelchair. Those were Dorothy's good days. On her bad days she, like many Alzheimer's patients, slapped and screamed at the people—to her, all strangers—who tried to help her.

With sadness enveloping the once active, happy world of the Aunt Hill and nearby Rydal Mount, Sarah Coleridge left the home that had been her refuge for so many years. She lived for a while with her son Derwent, in Cornwall. But then came exciting news from Sara and Henry, who were living in Hampstead, the upscale part of London that had been home to Leigh Hunt and John Keats: Sara was pregnant. Her mother moved in with the young couple and helped her daughter—her Frettikins—through the pregnancy, and then with the new baby. Then the Coleridge family curse struck again. Sara was tired, depressed, just generally not feeling well after having the baby. The prescription: opium. Opium and Coleridge blood made for a bad combination. Like her father, Sara tried to stop taking the drug once she started feeling better. But it had a hold on her, just as it had had on her father.

Hampstead held another attraction for Sarah Coleridge. It bordered on Highgate, also one of London's pleasant outskirts.

Dora Wordsworth

And Highgate was where Samuel Taylor Coleridge was living, alongside his constant watchman, Dr. Gillman. Sarah and Samuel were still married, although it had been many years since they had lived together as man and wife. Sarah had never given up on her husband, as so many people had. She had been his moral support when everyone else had abandoned him as hopeless, as a man unsalvageable, unworthy, unlovable. Samuel's obsession with Asra Hutchinson, the one person who had truly stood between them, was long over. The friendship between Sarah and Samuel strengthened; they bonded and reconciled, although they would never again live as a couple.

Sara Coleridge had broken free of the Lakes. It was harder for Dora Wordsworth. For one thing, it fell to her as the unmarried daughter, and not to her upwardly mobile brothers, to take care of her elderly parents and aunt at Rydal Mount. For another, Dora might be hot-tempered and smart, but as she grew older, it became apparent that her health was not good. Still, there were suitors for the blond "beautiful Cat of the Mountains," even after she turned thirty and was well past marrying age. Those suitors had to be uncommonly special, and uncommonly determined, to get past a barrier like William Wordsworth.

Maybe some sad news from London softened his heart, reminded him what passion and love were all about, and helped him reconsider the lonely future Dora would have ahead of her as a spinster. Early in the morning of July 25, 1834, Samuel Taylor Coleridge, age sixty-one, died at his home in Highgate. "The most *wonderful* man" William Wordsworth had ever known, his friend, his collaborator, a part of his very soul, was gone.

THE SOLITARY REAPER

by William Wordsworth

Behold her, single in the field,
Yon solitary Highland Lass!
Reaping and singing by herself;
Stop here, or gently pass!
Alone she cuts and binds the grain,
And sings a melancholy strain;
O listen! for the Vale profound
Is overflowing with the sound.

No Nightingale did ever chaunt
More welcome notes to weary bands
Of travelers in some shady haunt,
Among Arabian sands;
A voice so thrilling ne'er was heard
In springtime from the Cuckoo bird,
Breaking the silence of the seas
Among the farthest Hebrides.

Will no one tell me what she sings?—
Perhaps the plaintive numbers flow
For old, unhappy, far-off things,
And battles long ago;
Or is it some more humble lay,
Familiar matter of today?
Some natural sorrow, loss, or pain,
That has been, and may be again?

Whate'er the theme, the Maiden sang
As if her song could have no ending;
I saw her singing at her work,
And o'er the sickle bending—
I listened, motionless and still;
And, as I mounted up the hill,
The music in my heart I bore,
Long after it was heard no more.

WE ARE SEVEN

by William Wordsworth

————A simple Child,
That lightly draws its breath,
And feels its life in every limb,
What should it know of death?

I met a little cottage Girl:
She was eight years old, she said;
Her hair was thick with many a curl
That clustered round her head.

She had a rustic, woodland air,
And she was wildly clad:
Her eyes were fair, and very fair;
—Her beauty made me glad.

"Sisters and brothers, little Maid,
How many may you be?"
"How many? Seven in all," she said,
And wondering looked at me.

"And where are they? I pray you tell."
She answered, "Seven are we;
And two of us at Conway dwell,
And two are gone to sea.

"Two of us in the church-yard lie,
My sister and my brother;
And, in the church-yard cottage, I
Dwell near them with my mother."

"You say that two at Conway dwell,
And two are gone to sea,
Yet ye are seven!—I pray you tell,
Sweet Maid, how this may be."

Then did the little Maid reply,
"Seven boys and girls are we;
Two of us in the church-yard lie,
Beneath the church-yard tree."

"You run about, my little Maid,
Your limbs they are alive;
If two are in the church-yard laid,
Then ye are only five."

"Their graves are green, they may be seen,"
The little Maid replied,
"Twelve steps or more from my mother's door,
And they are side by side.

"My stockings there I often knit,
My kerchief there I hem;

And there upon the ground I sit,
And sing a song to them.

"And often after sunset, Sir,
When it is light and fair,
I take my little porringer,
And eat my supper there.

"The first that died was sister Jane;
In bed she moaning lay,
Till God released her of her pain;
And then she went away.

"So in the church-yard she was laid;
And, when the grass was dry,
Together round her grave we played,
My brother John and I.

"And when the ground was white with snow,
And I could run and slide,
My brother John was forced to go,
And he lies by her side."

"How many are you, then," said I,
"If they two are in heaven?"
Quick was the little Maid's reply,
"O Master! we are seven."

"But they are dead; those two are dead!
Their spirits are in heaven!"
'Twas throwing words away; for still
The little Maid would have her will,
And said, "Nay, we are seven!"

William Wordsworth

End of an Era

"Anchored on Everlasting Rest"

*T*he primary creator of *Lyrical Ballads,* the book that had spearheaded the Romantic movement in England, the book that had inspired Byron, Shelley, and Keats, was the last of them left. And he was a legend in his own time.

The English Lake District has always attracted visitors. It is a wildly beautiful place, and one can easily see how it could inspire so many poets. Wordsworth was so determined to keep the Lakes in pristine condition that he vehemently opposed the plan to extend rail service into the area.

But while Wordsworth was living in the region, the sapphire lakes and rocky, gorse-covered hills were not the only things people went up there to see. They went there to see *him,* "the wandering poet of Winandermere." People flocked to the homes where he'd lived and worked as if they were stops along Hollywood's Star Trail. One visitor begged a servant to be allowed into the poet's study. He wanted to see what sort of books surrounded a man like Wordsworth while he was at work. The servant, a little confused, led him to a room and said, "This is his library, but he *studies* in the fields."

The people looking for Wordsworth, and for mementos of the other Romantic poets, were not just tourists. Wordsworth had always been good at attracting an entourage, and he was still at it. American poets like Ralph Waldo Emerson traveled to England with the express desire to meet him. Alfred, Lord Tennyson, signed the autograph book Dora Wordsworth kept at Rydal Mount. Elizabeth Barrett was also among Wordsworth's visitors. A teenager with literary aspirations, Branwell Brontë, hoped to strike up a correspondence with the elderly poet. He wrote Wordsworth a letter that must have brought back memories of Coleridge on one of his worst days. Wordsworth didn't reply.

Those Romantic ideas had been revolutionary when Wordsworth and Coleridge had first written them down, back in the waning days of the eighteenth century. Now, in Wordsworth's old age, they were so accepted that they had become part of the curriculum for many schools. Editions of his poems were being specially packaged for use in the classroom.

Maybe it was because he was the last one alive. Or maybe it was because he looked and lived like a respectable gentleman— he wasn't a drug addict, an atheist, a pervert, or lower-class, like those others had been. Whatever the reason, Wordsworth found himself being invited to recite in classrooms in a nineteenth-century version of Author Day. In one school he visited, the boys recited his old sonnet, "Westminster Bridge." Then they analyzed its imagery and debated its meaning—with its poet right there to guide them.

Robert Southey's death had created an opening for the position of poet laureate of England. The job paid a comfortable sum of money—which had been Southey's main concern—as well as honor and glory. And it wasn't a terribly strenuous position, which was fortunate for Wordsworth, since his eyesight was failing and writing was getting harder and harder. Wordsworth agreed to succeed Southey as laureate—and he was only called upon to perform his official duty of writing a poem as requested by the Crown once. It was nothing special, just something to commemorate some royal function in 1847. Its only claim to fame is that it is Wordsworth's last published poem.

Coleridge's death must have softened the old man when it came to his daughter, Dora, still unmarried, still hoping to find love—and starting to show the first symptoms of tuberculosis. Finally, one of Dora Wordsworth's suitors was allowed to approach. He was not the man William might have chosen for his daughter. But Dorothy was all for the match, when her mind was clear, and so was Wordsworth's good friend, Isabella Fenwick. William Quillinan, Dora's future husband, had certainly been persistent and determined: They had been friends for twenty years. Quillinan was a widower with two children—and, even worse for an ultra-conservative like Wordsworth, a Catholic. Finally, in 1841, the two were married at Isabella Fenwick's home in Bath. William Wordsworth did not attend the wedding. Then, as worried about Dora's failing health as her own parents were, Quillinan whisked his bride away to the warm, sunny climate of Portugal. Dora only enjoyed the marriage she'd waited for so long for six years. She died of tuberculosis in 1847.

William and Mary Wordsworth were also worrying about one of their other children. It wasn't John, the one with the learning disability. He'd settled down as a minister. It was young William—Willie. He just couldn't get a job and hold on to it; he had no desire to work. When his father had been his age, he hadn't been working, either. He'd been busy becoming a ground-breaking poet. But there was a difference. William Sr. had been lucky enough to find patrons who would support his writing. And he'd had blazing talent. The only people Willie could count on for money were his parents, and his father hadn't passed along the poetry gene. All William could do for his son was call in some favors to get him a nice, undemanding job—like his old position of stamp distributor.

The Wordsworth family also continued to watch the heart-breaking deterioration of Hartley Coleridge. William might be the wandering poet of Winandermere, but Hartley was its wandering alcoholic derelict. The Wordsworths hadn't been able to help Hartley's father, and they were unable to pull the son together. He finally died in January of 1849, and the Wordsworths did the one thing they could. They buried him alongside their own family, in the Grasmere churchyard.

Down in London, Sara Coleridge and her mother were doing what they could to salvage Sam's reputation. Sarah had put out a newspaper advertisement soon after her husband's death: Could anyone who had letters, papers, any sort of correspondence from S.T.C., please send it to her? If it portrayed him as an out-of-control, crazed drug fiend, she destroyed it. If it was more positive, she passed it on to her daughter. Sara, the only one of Coleridge's children with a fraction of his genius, was determined to sift through her father's voluminous, largely unfinished work and edit it. She kept at the job until she died of breast cancer in 1852, at the age of forty-nine.

There were no real happy endings for the children of the Romantic poets. Augusta Ada Byron inherited her mother's mathematical genius. Charles Babbage is the man who gets the credit for inventing a prototype computer in the 1800s. His assistant isn't mentioned quite as often—but that assistant was Ada Byron. Unfortunately, she was also touched by the curse of the Romantics: an addiction to opium.

Herbert Coleridge, the poet's grandson, looked like he might have inherited the Coleridge genius without its fatal flaws. Like his grandfather, he was a polymath—a person fascinated by, and skilled in, just about anything and everything. His grandfather had dreamed of compiling an encyclopedia; Herbert was involved at the start of the project that would become the

Oxford English Dictionary. But cold and damp, and Romantic poets and their relatives, don't mix. Herbert Coleridge died after sitting through a lecture in an unheated hall, soaked to the skin from the pouring rain he'd run through to get there.

Walking had defined William Wordsworth's life. And, ultimately, it played a part in his death.

William was still tramping up and down the wild hills of the Lake District in his fifties, then his sixties. When he was seventy, he climbed to the top of Helvellyn, one of the area's highest peaks. As a young man, he'd disregarded bad weather. But the winter of 1850 was very cold; still, William Wordsworth insisted on going out for a nice long walk. He came home chilled and developed pleurisy, a serious lung condition.

While William was sick, a sort of miracle happened at Rydal Mount. For years, Dorothy had been living in a shadow world of dementia. Yet when her brother took to his bed, Dorothy got out of hers and suddenly began running the household—and quite competently. But as she felt better, he grew worse. Mary Wordsworth whispered to her husband that soon, soon, he'd be enjoying a nice long visit with his beloved Dora.

At noon on April 13, 1850, the little bird sprang out of the cuckoo clock Isabella Fenwick had given to the Wordsworths. And the family, gathered at William's bedside, watched him draw his last breath.

Other poets would carry on the ideas of the first Romantics: their fascination with genuine emotion, with lyrical use of everyday language, with ordinary people and ordinary situations. But within a generation, it was a tradition. For Wordsworth and Coleridge, for Byron and Shelley and Keats, Romanticism had meant *breaking* with tradition. Theirs was an experiment in wildness, in craziness, in the audaciousness of being the first to try something so new. It wasn't enough for them to write in a Romantic style. Theirs were the ultimate Romantic lives.

The Poems

COMPOSED UPON WESTMINSTER BRIDGE
by William Wordsworth

Earth has not anything to show more fair:
Dull would he be of soul who could pass by
A sight so touching in its majesty;
This City now doth, like a garment, wear
The beauty of the morning; silent, bare,
Ships, towers, domes, theaters, and temples lie
Open unto the fields, and to the sky;
All bright and glittering in the smokeless air.
Never did sun more beautifully steep
In his first splendor, valley, rock, or hill;
Ne'er saw I, never felt, a calm so deep!
The river glideth at his own sweet will:
Dear God! the very houses seem asleep;
And all that mighty heart is lying still!

PRAYER FOR TRANQUILLITY

by Sara Coleridge

Dear Lord, who, at thy blessed will,
Didst make the raging wind be still,
And smooth the tossing of the Sea,
Oh! cause our stormy griefs to flee,
Our wild tempestuous thoughts allay,
And fires of passion send away.
Conduct us here to perfect peace,
When all our earthly transports cease,
And lastly, while to Thee we cling,
Our souls to that blest haven bring,
Above the sphere of Care and Woe
Where earthly blasts can never blow,
With Thee to dwell, supremely blest,
Anchored on everlasting rest.

Chapter Notes

Wordsworth

Esteesi

Lyrical Balladeers

51 "Had I met these lines . . .'Wordsworth!' "—Holmes, *Coleridge: Early Visions,* p. 214

A LIFE IN RUINS

62 "As to Poetry . . . original power"—Jones, p. 106

63 "He likes to have . . . it was all over"—Lefebure, p. 195.

63 "Have you taken too much or too little opium?"—Lefebure, p. 197

68 "Wordsworth has given me up"—Bate, *Coleridge,* p. 195

68 "Wordsworth and his sister . . . his own reputation"—Lefebure, p. 132

68 "excellent air-bag"—Jones, p. 83

68 "an Archangel a little damaged"—Holmes, *Coleridge: Darker Reflections,* p. 430

BABY BYRON

83 "the Devil . . . without my description"—Letter from Byron to his solicitor, John Hanson, 11/23/1805, www.poemhunter.com

85 "That is Greece . . . *that* is England"—Raphael, p. 38

88 "I awoke one morning and found myself famous"—Trease, p. 69

89 "I have been . . . men like scarecrows"—Trease, pp. 68–69

YOUNG SHELLEY

96 "And water . . . pass by thee"—Southey, Robert, "The Curse of Kehama," www.wwnorton.com/nto/romantic/topic_4/southey.htm

98 "My son here has a literary turn . . printing freaks"—Tomalin, p. 16

99 "We must live I suppose on love"—Holmes, *Shelley: The Pursuit,* p. 78

101 "such a lunatic angel, such a ruined man"—Spark, p. 218

103 "Bysshe looked . . . out of the ground"—Holmes, *Shelley: The Pursuit,* p. 172

104 "I expect no success . . . their sons and daughters may"—Holmes, *Shelley: The Pursuit,* p. 189

MARY GODWIN

116 "You love a perpetual sparkle and glittering"—Holmes, *Shelley: The Pursuit,* p. 181

119 "All his poems are the same poem with a different title"—St. Clair, p. 340

BYRONIC ENTANGLEMENTS

124 "mad, bad, and dangerous to know"—Blyth, p. 88

124 "Your heart, my poor Caro . . . lives now"—Blyth, p. 113

125 "I should like her more if she were less perfect"—Eisler, p. 357

126 "I thank you again . . . never to meet"—Trease, p. 75

127 "You have told . . . an Englishwoman can"—Blyth, p. 144

128 "Do, my dear. But . . . struck there already"—Blyth, p. 153

128 "I mean to use this.". . ."Against me, I presume"—Blyth, p. 153

129 "Remember thee . . . *fiend* to me"—Blyth, pp. 155–156

130 "Good God, I am surely in hell"—Eisler, p. 451

130 "I have great hopes . . . married at all"—Letter, 12/5/1814,
       www.poemhunter.com

133 "All convulsions end with me in rhyme"—Trueblood, p. 57

133 "I can never get people . . . such a state?"—Letter, 7/5/1821,
       www.poemhunter.com

134 "a torture . . . a great pain"—Grosskurth, p. 377

135 "If a woman . . . silent as the grave?"—Grosskurth, p. 265

136 "I felt that, if what was whispered . . . unfit for me"—Grosskurth, p. 260

BYRON AND SHELLEY AND THE GIRLS

141 "a fire in his eye . . . fluttering in his speech"—Motion, p. 139

142 "He says he is unhappy. God in heaven what has he to be unhappy about!"—
       Holmes, *Shelley: The Pursuit,* p. 268

142 "All the ladies would say 'Look at that poor Byron, how interesting he looks
       in dying' "—Motion, p. 499

143 "democrat, great lover of mankind and atheist."—Tomalin, p. 58

145 "Methinks it is a wonderful work for a girl of nineteen,—*not* nineteen,
       indeed, at that time"—Spark, p. 154

KEATS

158 "There was a naughty Boy . . . and he wonder'd"—Bate, *Keats,* p. 69

160 "Did our great Poets ever write short pieces?"—Bate, *Keats,* p. 74

160 "does say true things now and then"—Motion, p. 543

161 "evidence of insanity"—Motion, p. 57

161 "a pretty piece of Paganism"—Bate, *Keats,* p. 265

161 "To W. Wordsworth with the Author's sincere Reverence"—Watts, p. 29

163 "Yes, I believe, Mr. Keats, we may admire these works safely"—Bate, *Keats,* p. 247

164 "Keats did not take . . . natural enemy"—Motion, p. 139

164 "mental masturbation"—Eisler, p. 683

165 "I go among the . . . one human heart"—Watts, p. 103

167 "I have got wet through day after day . . . many things else"—Watts, p. 38

168 "[She] is I think beautiful . . . acting stylishly"—Bate, *Keats,* p. 424

169 "How beautiful the season is . . . composed upon it"—Bate, *Keats,* p. 580

170 "There is death in that hand"—Bate, *Keats,* p. 468

170 "I know the colour of that blood . . . I must die"—Motion, p. 496

170 "making [his] exit like a frog in a frost . . . I cannot bear to leave her"—Bate, *Keats,* p. 640

172 "Where is Keats now? . . . an added pleasure"—Motion, p. 524

173 "This gives me the most horrid idea . . . human misery"—Motion, p. 545

174 "posthumous existence"—Motion, p. 556

175 "fairy lamplighter"—Motion, p. 563

175 "For Three weeks I have never . . . with the want of every proper material"—Bate, *Keats,* p. 684

177 "Here lies one whose name was writ in water."—Watts, p. 60

177 "This Grave contains . . . Tomb Stone"—Watts, p. 60

177 "John Keats . . . an article"—Byron, "Don Juan," canto 11, verse 60, "Lord Byron: Selected Poetry," http://englishhistory.net/byron/poetry.html

DEAD BABIES

190 "Don't look at him. . . . He is dangerous to look at"—Trease, p. 117

190 "as mad as the winds—Eisler, p. 524

191 "will do more harm to the English character, than anything of our time"—Grosskurth, p. 339

191 "Satanic school"—Trueblood, p. 112

191 "The reading or non-reading a book will never keep down a single petticoat"—Letter, 10/20/1819, www.poemhunter.com

192 "smell so of garlic"—Eisler, p. 599

Sources

Borrowers of books—those mutilators of collections, spoilers of the symmetry of shelves, and creators of odd volumes.

—Charles Lamb

Bate, Walter Jackson. *Coleridge*. New York: Macmillan, 1968.

————. *John Keats*. Cambridge, MA: Belknap Press, 1963.

Blyth, Henry. *Caro: The Fatal Passion: The Life of Lady Caroline Lamb*. New York: Coward, McCann and Geoghegan, 1972.

Bober, Natalie. *William Wordsworth: The Wandering Poet*. New York: Thomas Nelson, 1975.

Davies, Hunter. *William Wordsworth: A Biography*. New York: Atheneum, 1980.

Eisler, Benita. *Byron: Child of Passion, Fool of Fame*. New York: Alfred A. Knopf, 1999.

Gill, Stephen. *William Wordsworth: A Life*. Oxford: Clarendon Press, 1989.

"Great Books Online." www.bartleby.com.

Grosskurth, Phyllis. *Byron: The Flawed Angel*. Boston: Houghton Mifflin, 1997.

Holmes, Richard. *Coleridge: Darker Reflections, 1804–1834*. New York: Pantheon, 1998.

————. *Coleridge: Early Visions, 1772–1804*. New York: Viking, 1989.

————. *Shelley: The Pursuit*. New York: Penguin Books, 1987.

Jones, Kathleen. *A Passionate Sisterhood: The Sisters, Wives and Daughters of the Lake Poets*. New York: St. Martin's Press, 2000.

Lefebure, Molly. *The Bondage of Love: A Life of Mrs. Samuel Taylor Coleridge*. New York: W. W. Norton, 1986.

Mahoney, John L. *William Wordsworth: A Poetic Life*. New York: Fordham University Press, 1997.

Mellor, Anne K. *Mary Shelley: Her Life, Her Fiction, Her Monsters*. New York: Methuen, 1988.

Motion, Andrew. *Keats*. New York: Farrar, Straus and Giroux, 1997.

The Norton Anthology of English Literature. Volume 2, 3rd edition. New York: W. W. Norton, 1974.

"Poemhunter." www.poemhunter.com.

Raphael, Frederic. *Byron*. New York: Thames and Hudson, 1982.

Spark, Muriel. *Mary Shelley*. New York: E. P. Dutton, 1987.

St. Clair, William. *The Godwins and the Shelleys: A Biography of a Family*. New York: W. W. Norton, 1989.

Tomalin, Claire. *Shelley and His World*. New York: Charles Scribner's Sons, 1980.

Trease, Geoffrey. *Byron: A Poet Dangerous to Know*. New York: Holt, Rinehart and Winston, 1969.

Trueblood, Paul Graham. *Lord Byron*. Boston: Twayne Publishers, 1969.

Watts, Cedric, ed. *A Preface to Keats*. New York: Longman, 1985.

Winchester, Simon. *The Professor and the Madman: A Tale of Murder, Insanity, and the Making of the* Oxford English Dictionary. New York: HarperCollins, 1998.

For Further Reading and Viewing

Bloom, Harold, ed. *English Romantic Poetry*. New York: Chelsea House, 2004.

————. *George Gordon, Lord Byron*. New York: Chelsea House, 2004.

————. *John Keats*. New York: Chelsea House, 2001.

————. *Mary Shelley*. New York: Chelsea House, 1985.

————. *Percy Bysshe Shelley: Comprehensive Research and Study Guide*. New York: Chelsea House, 2001.

————. *Samuel T. Coleridge: Comprehensive Research and Study Guide*. New York: Chelsea House, 2001.

————. *William Wordsworth*. New York: Chelsea House, 2003.

Coleridge, Samuel Taylor. *The Rime of the Ancient Mariner*. Illustrated by Ed Young. New York: Atheneum, 1992.

Cook, Elizabeth, ed. *John Keats: Selected Poetry*. Oxford: Oxford University Press, 1998.

Duane, O. B. *Byron: Passionate Romantic*. London: Brockhampton Press, 1998.

Engell, James, ed. *Samuel Taylor Coleridge*. New York: Sterling, 2003.

Hoobler, Dorothy, and Thomas Hoobler. *The Monsters: Mary Shelley and the Curse of Frankenstein*. Boston: Little, Brown & Co., 2006.

King, Neil. *The Romantics: English Literature in Its Historical, Cultural, and Social Contexts*. New York: Facts on File, 2003.

Kirkpatrick, Patricia. *John Keats*. Illustrated by Etienne Delessert. Mankato, MN: Creative Education, 2006.

Liu, Alan. *Poetry for Young People: William Wordsworth*. Illustrated by James Muir. New York: Sterling, 2003.

Miller, Calvin Craig. *Spirit Like a Storm: The Story of Mary Shelley*. Greensboro, NC: Morgan Reynolds, 2003.

The Romantic Poets. Videorecording; written by David Manson; produced by Lara Lowe. West Long Branch, NJ: Kultur, 1999.

Shelley, Mary Wollstonecraft. *Frankenstein*. New York: Signet Classics, 2000.

Sullivan, K. E. *Coleridge: Lyrical Romantic*. London: Brockhampton Press, 1998.

————. *Wordsworth: The Eternal Romantic*. London: Brockhampton Press, 1996.

Thompson, James R. *Leigh Hunt*. Boston: Twayne, 1977.

INDEX OF POEMS

INDEX

(Page references in *italic* refer to illustrations.)